WHAT THEY

Don't

TEACH YOU
AT THE
MTC

WHAT THEY
Don't
TEACH YOU
AT THE
MTC

NORMAN C. HILL

CFI

SPRINGVILLE, UT

Dedication

To Raelene

Who can find a virtuous woman? She is far above rubies,
her children and husband rise up and call her blessed, and her
own works shall praise her (Proverbs 3:10, 28–31).

To Stephanie

Who gives me beauty for ashes, the joy of oil for mourning, and the
garment of praise for the spirit of heaviness (Isaiah 61:3).

Contents

CONTENTS

I HOPE THEY CALL ME
ON A MISSION

Get ready, get set . . .

We often belt out with gusto the Primary song "I Hope They Call Me on a Mission." We know it, we sing it, we love it. Elder M. Russell Ballard likes the song too and wants us to take it to heart as we sing it. "Young people need to commit themselves early in life to the idea of a mission."[1] However, knowing you need to serve a mission and feeling prepared to serve are two different things. Where do you start?

Various online resources and Church manuals can assist you, but *Preach My Gospel* is the fundamental guide to missionary service. It contains basic principles and authorized materials for teaching gospel lessons to friends and acquaintances. Introduced in 2004, it was updated in 2018. Updates in the 2018 version reflect additional direction from Church leaders and changes to the missionary program in the fourteen years since *Preach My Gospel* was first released. This elaborate resource contains fundamental principles for helping missionaries find, teach, and baptize. In addition, "the lessons and principles contained in it will help people become disciples of the Lord Jesus Christ."[2]

Today's prospective missionaries are often well-versed in the scriptures, but they face unprecedented societal challenges: depression and anxiety are commonplace among teens and young adults; normal peer

1

pressure is aggravated by social media comparisons and cyberbullying; and health pandemics and social unrest seem to promote generational differences. With these many hindrances, are young men and women in the Church today of the ages of eighteen or nineteen acquiring the maturity, social skills, and work habits they will need "to teach and preach and work as missionaries do"?

ARE THEY READY?

I was a mission president when researchers asked me that question. When the age requirements for missionary service were changed, eighteen-year-old young men and nineteen-year-old young women began arriving in our mission. My response to the question was similar to the response of other mission presidents. We explained that most of these new missionaries were well prepared spiritually, but gaps in other areas of their lives created challenges for them. Many found it difficult to live on their own, especially in a new country. In fact, even missionaries who were a few years older often had difficulty adapting to the rigors of the missionary schedule and the challenges of a new, unfamiliar culture. However, we explained that with time, patience, and concerted effort these gaps could be closed.

Reading about missionary service and discussing it in Church meetings is one thing. But the reality of getting up each morning at 6:30 a.m. and living the missionary life day after day is quite another. So, what does it take to help new and prospective missionaries cycle through these challenges more quickly, hit the ground running sooner, adapt to the rigors of missionary work more smoothly, and minimize trial and error methods?

A COMPANION TO *PREACH MY GOSPEL*

This collection of stories, experiences, and advice from Church leaders, mission presidents, missionaries, and researchers is designed to answer that question and fill noticeable gaps. It is based on *Preach My Gospel* and provides practical suggestions for using principles outlined in that resource guide. This book utilizes *Preach My Gospel* as the foundational guide for all missionary activity. Built on that solid foundation, it takes important principles and expounds, enriches, and enhances them.

Some years ago, I was asked to write a book about repentance, using practical examples and applications to accompany *The Miracle of Forgiveness* by President Spencer W. Kimball. The publisher didn't want another version of doctrinal matters on repentance and forgiveness—they were already well covered in President Kimball's book. Instead the publisher wanted a book on how to apply those principles in everyday life. I wrote *The Road Back* to share real life stories and examples of how ordinary Saints use "godly sorrow" as a catalyst to find strength in vulnerability when confessing and forsaking their sins, forgiving and moving on when offended, and otherwise continuing on the covenant path despite enormous obstacles.

PRACTICAL APPLICATIONS

Like *The Road Back*, this book is about practical applications. It is primarily for prospective full-time missionaries but can be used by wards and branches in developing ward and branch mission plans, coordinating missionary efforts, and fully implementing *Preach My Gospel*. Here is what is unique about this book:

- It takes principles identified in *Preach My Gospel* and *Adjusting to Missionary Life* and develops them into practical applications.
- It describes how to use new tools and methods for fellowshipping and online contacting that are now being introduced at missions throughout the world.
- It vets practical research on personal relationships and teaching methods encouraged in *Teaching in the Savior's Way* and *Come Follow Me*.

When Elder David A. Bednar of the Quorum of the Twelve Apostles was a member of the Church's Missionary Committee, he emphasized that too often prospective or current missionaries mistake memorization for studying, and confuse telling with teaching. "We [should] understand that talking and telling alone are not teaching," he said. "Preaching the gospel the Lord's way includes observing and listening and discerning as prerequisites to talking."[3]

These critical missionary skills—observing, listening, and discerning—are further explored and explained throughout *What They Don't Teach You at the MTC,* along with a review of practical suggestions of how to apply them in everyday missionary settings. This book also shares the surprising evidence-based *emotional* benefits of such activities as baking, making your bed, and sticking to a schedule despite rainy days or quarantines. Additionally, it discusses practical ways to become a virtual missionary, use visual aids creatively in teaching, and learn interactively. In clear and concise language, rich with metaphors and personal experiences, this book adds to the who, what, why, and how of the principles and doctrines presented in *Preach My Gospel.*

PREPARE IN ADVANCE

Missionary Training Centers do a marvelous job in preparing elders and sisters to serve. They provide an introduction to full-time missionary service that includes inspirational talks from Church leaders, excerpts from *Preach My Gospel,* and, when required, foreign language training. But because of time limitations, they can only do so much.

Prospective missionaries who prepare in advance can compress the missionary learning curve, smooth out rough edges, and develop the "finer points" of proselyting, that might otherwise take an extended period of time to attain once they arrive in the mission field, or potentially get missed altogether. Prepare now to make the most of your mission by learning those extra things that can make all the difference between success and failure, such as:

- Getting along with companions instead of counting the days until a transfer.
- Teaching with the Spirit instead of stumbling along on your own.
- Really thriving rather than merely surviving.

In recent years, Church leaders have often stressed the need for such preparation. President Russell M. Nelson said, "Preparation for a mission is important. . . . A desire to serve is a natural outcome of one's conversion, worthiness, and preparation."[4]

Of course you will make study, prayer, and Church participation part of your preparation. But you can also prepare yourself by learning to:

- Develop relationships of trust though making and keeping commitments.
- Make decisions based on good habits and character traits, not simply feelings or emotional impressions.
- Profit from experience, even tough experiences.
- Become undeterred by insincere flattery or unjust criticism.
- Gain an understanding of others needs and what it means to put people ahead of your own interests.
- Grow into being a self-starter who knows how to live independently.

INDIRECT LEARNING

These are *learned* traits. They can be acquired through *indirect learning*—by noticing what others do and how they do it. Indirect learning is observing and imitating the effective ways others do things.

Suppose you notice that several of your friends sit in a chair when studying, use note cards and review them often, and then seem to remember better than others what they have read. You decide to imitate them, so you give up lying on your bed and listening to music through headphones while studying. After a while, you find that you too are remembering more of what you read and study.

That's indirect learning. When learning from others you have to be certain to properly assess what you have learned so that you don't misinterpret a situation and come up with the wrong actions. Indirect learning requires practice and close observation to ensure that you are able to draw the right conclusions. For example, if someone is doing something that works, check it out. But check it out in various situations, and with several different people to ensure you have assessed what really works and produces desired results.

THE HARDEST TWO YEARS?

Shortly after the missionary age was lowered, the Church provided to all newly called missionaries a booklet called *Adjusting to Missionary Life*. This resource guide acknowledges the many physical, social, emotional, intellectual, and spiritual challenges faced by newly called missionaries and full-time missionaries in general. It provides a brief personal assessment questionnaire and ways for coping with stress.

The introduction to this guidebook notes:

> "Even with a promise of the Lord's help, many of the greatest missionaries in history recorded that they suffered and struggled in their missionary labors. Ammon and his brethren 'suffer[ed] much, both in body and in mind, such as hunger, thirst and fatigue, and also much labor in the spirit' (Alma 17:5). At times, they apparently wanted to go home. 'Now when our hearts were depressed, and we were about to turn back, behold, the Lord comforted us, and said: Go amongst thy brethren, the Lamanites, and bear with patience thine afflictions, and I will give unto you success' (Alma 26:27)." [5]

Calling on the Lord helped these Book of Mormon missionaries anciently, and calling on Him today will help you just as much. It is His work, and we must do it in His way. But you must also do your part. It is not enough to want to learn how to be an effective missionary; you must put those desires into action and learn by study and by faith, by observing and listening, by practicing and discerning.

Elder Bednar has written much and taught often about learning. He notes that we often discuss the skills of a teacher teaching more often than the skills of a learner learning, and emphasizes that learning is hard work, requiring much more than merely paying attention to a teacher: "A learner exercising agency by acting in accordance with correct principles opens his or her heart to the Holy Ghost and invites His teaching, testifying power, and confirming witness. Learning by faith requires spiritual, mental, and physical exertion and not just passive reception."[6]

As we learn from others, we fundamentally develop our own personal resilience and become more spiritually and emotionally well-grounded. We gain a better perspective on life, and the need for the work of the Lord not only here and now but also in the scope of eternity. In preparing for missionary service, you will recognize that you are part of something much bigger than yourself. While missionary work can be satisfying when we see others accept the gospel, get baptized, and continue on the path toward eternal life, it can also be difficult. The "two best years of your life" may also be two of the hardest. However, if you make the most of your opportunity to serve, the personal growth you experience will be phenomenal.

BEGIN WITH THE END IN MIND

I had the privilege of working as a research and teaching assistant for Stephen R. Covey when he was a university professor. In addition to discussing research methods, we often talked about gospel topics. He had served as a mission president in Ireland, and he told me that in his first interview with new missionaries he asked them both to dedicate themselves to their full-time service and to begin with the end in mind. This included deciding what kind of missionary they intended to be as well as what kind of parent they intended to become, what kind of Church member they would aspire to be, and what kind of lifelong commitments they were willing to make right then and there. He asked them to plan for their re-entry back to their home, even as they took their first steps in missionary life. He told his new missionaries to "become the disciple your Heavenly Father wants and expects you to become, and plan your re-entry back home accordingly." When he asked missionaries to imagine returning home, he asked them to consider a mission as another step in their eternal progress, not just a discrete activity they would complete in 24 or 18 months.

Every prospective missionary, and every missionary who is currently serving, would benefit by seeing their mission with that lifelong perspective. It's a perspective that will help you answer questions like:

- What kind of stories will you have to tell from your mission?
- What kind of obstacles will you likely face and how will you address them?
- How will you use your mission to help you determine a career path?
- How will you stay on the covenant path throughout your life?

These are important questions, and Brother Covey thought it was helpful even for brand new missionaries to think about them at the start of their mission. In fact, he thought it was absolutely essential that they do so.

Sometimes missionaries say that a mission is the "MTC for life," almost as if it is a framework for the future. Lehi's vision of the Tree of Life recognizes that mortality is a journey, and moving forward is an essential feature of Heavenly Father's plan. Seeing the ultimate goal helps us to stay on track. So, this book also includes material for returning missionaries and senior missionaries, as well as material for younger missionaries, full-time missionaries, and ward missionaries.

Elder Dieter F. Uchtdorf of the Quorum of the Twelve Apostles often compares life to an adventure filled with both challenges and opportunities. "If you hesitate in this adventure because you doubt your ability, remember that discipleship is not about doing things perfectly; it's about doing things intentionally. It is your choices that show what you truly are, far more than your abilities."[7]

YOU CAN DO IT!

Heavenly Father wants you to be happy. He won't ask you to do things that won't bless your life. If you faithfully do what the Lord asks of you, even when it's hard, you'll find that the blessings that come are way better than anything you could've imagined. You'll never regret serving a mission.

REFERENCES

1. M. Russell Ballard, "How to Prepare to Be a Good Missionary," *New Era,* March 2007, 6.
2. "Updated Version of Preach My Gospel Now Available," *Church News,* June 22, 2018, churchofjesuschrist.org/church/news/updated-version-of-preach-my-gospel-now-available?lang=eng.
3. David A. Bednar, "Becoming a *Preach My Gospel* Missionary," *New Era,* October 2013, 6.
4. Russell M. Nelson, "Ask the Missionaries! They Can Help You!" *Ensign,* November 2012, 18.
5. *Adjusting to Missionary Life,* The Church of Jesus Christ of Latter-day Saints (manual, 2013), 1, churchofjesuschrist.org/study/manual/resource-booklet-adjusting-to-missionary-life/introduction.
6. David A. Bednar, "Seek Learning by Faith," *Ensign,* September 2007, 64.
7. Dieter F. Uchtdorf, "Your Great Adventure," *Ensign,* November 2019, 37.

Chapter 2

THOSE OTHER SKILLS

Some things you may not realize that every missionary needs

I was teaching at the institute of religion, and had just finished the final missionary preparation class for the semester when a group of students gathered around me. They wanted to know the most important things they could do, even before submitting their missionary applications, to be prepared to serve. Their question reminded me of a similar question I received in a survey from the Missionary Department while I was serving as a mission president in Ghana. At that time, the Missionary Department wanted to know how to help eighteen-year-old young men and nineteen-year-old young women better prepare for missionary service—what did these young men and young women need most before embarking in the service of the Lord?

I gave the same answer to the institute students that I gave to the Missionary Department.

Most missionaries are prepared spiritually to one extent or another. Many have been to seminary and institute and have learned the gospel well. Many know the scriptures. Many understand the basic doctrines. They have held callings and have some experience knowing how the Church functions. Most know what it means to be guided by the Holy Ghost and have felt His gentle promptings.

What they often lack, however, are life skills.

Such skills can make the difference between enjoying a mission and the growth it brings, or feeling stressed and out of place. All missionaries go through a transition. But developing the proper life skills, more than any other preparation, can reduce frustration with everyday missionary tasks and provide resilience that helps in adjusting to missionary work. And there's a bonus: having appropriate life skills also enables the missionary to have more fun!

So what are these skills, and how are they developed? Which skills are important to learn before going out, can be learned while serving, and can be learned later? What life skills, if not gained before a mission, make adapting to missionary service much more difficult? Most importantly, can these life skills be taught and learned in a few short months before a mission if they have previously been neglected? This chapter answers those questions.

THE RIGHT WAY THROUGH THE RITE OF PASSAGE

It's hard to grow up. Entering adulthood is a challenging rite of passage regardless of the circumstances. For young missionaries who may be on their own for the first time in their lives, the transition from adolescence to adulthood can be especially intense. The good news is that critical life skills can be taught and learned in a short amount of time. By beginning to develop them before they embark on their missions, most missionaries will avoid the arrested development that can occur if these skills are ignored or put off until later.

Let's look at a couple of examples.

Elder Burgon (not his real name) came from a strong family and attended seminary throughout high school. His two older brothers had served missions. He attended a missionary preparation class before his call, so he knew to some degree what to expect on his mission. But he had never lived away from home. He wasn't used to making his own meals, doing his own laundry, or getting up early in the morning. He became discouraged easily when rejected by contacts or investigators. He was so overwhelmed with a rigorous, structured schedule that he had difficulty coping with daily missionary life and often found it difficult working with others. He even convinced his parents to send a video gaming system to him in the mail so he could relax with it in the evenings.

By contrast, Elder Driscoll (not his real name, either) came from a similar background—strong family, with lots of his own Church experience. But the summer before his call he had lived with an uncle in another town so he could better earn money for his mission. He had to get up early, work hard, and take care of his own personal needs, such as washing his clothes and preparing his own meals. When he arrived in the mission field, even though he had a difficult trainer in a foreign country, he adapted to these new circumstances because he had already mastered a few essential life skills.

WHAT YOU'LL NEED TO THRIVE WHEN YOU ARRIVE

Based on a survey of recently returned missionaries, here's a list of life skills needed before going on a mission.

1. ABILITY TO MANAGE TIME

There are dozens of books and hundreds of articles on time management. Methods often start with prioritizing what needs to be done and then developing a plan to accomplish it. It involves trying new things without expecting everything to go perfectly, then assessing results and making adjustments. But how does a would-be missionary get started?

I asked a group of recently returned missionaries what helped them most when it came to managing time. One of them, a country western music fan, told me that every morning when he woke up, he sang an old folk song by Roger Miller called "You Can't Roller Skate in a Buffalo Herd." The chorus says:

"All you gotta do is put your mind to it,
Knuckle down, buckle down, do it, do it, do it."

He said singing this song helped both him and his companions get started each day. Because it is a funny song, it lifted their spirits, helped them roll through bad weather or tough times, and prevented them from taking disappointments or even boredom too seriously. Singing a fun, upbeat song with a positive message was their antidote to the monotony of daily missionary life. It helped them make daily plans and then stick with them.

Start somewhere. Making a daily plan is a discipline that improves with effort and practice. What do you want to get done today? Make a list. Next, how are you going to get those things done? What are the steps you need to take? Write them down. How will you know when you've made progress or achieved your desired results? Write that down, too. Writing forces focus. Once you've written something down, it creates its own motivation. It becomes compelling. The same thing occurs when you write up a plan. Writing helps you take action. And the more often you create a daily plan, the more it becomes a habit.

Avoid procrastination. We can all fall into the trap of putting things off that need to get done. We avoid starting tasks that may be unpleasant, even if they are important. But for today's millennials, the biggest culprits that prevent daily planning are ordinary distractions—texting, phone calls, and random activities.

Paul Towers, a workplace consultant, says that multitasking lies at the core of procrastination for most young people because it is so activity driven. They receive a sense of accomplishment from texting, taking phone calls, and responding to other stimuli. However, multitasking is really procrastination disguised as action. It's like sitting in a car with the engine running, but never shifting into gear and driving down the street. To counteract the distraction of multi-tasking, focus on doing just one thing at a time. Prioritize tasks. Then focus on accomplishing them one at a time. That's time management at its finest.

2. ABILITY TO MANAGE MONEY

Setting up a bank account with a debit card is a good first step for understanding money management. It's a great way to learn that there's only so much money, and when it's gone, it's gone.

As a missionary you won't have cash, you'll have a debit card with a monthly amount for subsistence. What's "subsistence?" Each mission president, following some basic Missionary Department guidelines, determines how much missionaries in his mission should receive for food, transportation, and other needs. The amount varies by mission, based on variables such as whether or not rent and utilities are paid directly by the mission office or by the missionaries themselves. This subsistence amount is deposited into each missionary's account each month, and missionaries use a debit card to pay for ordinary expenses. They have to budget to have enough money to carry them through the month.

Those who have already mastered this money management life skill will have an easier time living on a subsistence budget. Rather than haphazardly spending money on anything that comes along, they will know how to plan for and pay daily expenses. It won't be a new experience; it will be something they're already used to doing.

People tend to make budgeting complex or overly detailed. That's the wrong approach. What works is being aware of where you spend money and deliberately deciding where you will spend it. You don't need detailed worksheets. Simply track your spending habits by recording expenses on a clean sheet of paper. Then, review expenses and spending at the end of each month together with your companion.

Keeping track of where you spend your money—all of it—is the single most important technique for learning to manage it well. Too often either we don't track our actual spending or expect that things will simply take care of themselves. We don't really know how to plan for various monthly expenses because we are absent-minded about where our money went. Fortunately, keeping track of where you spend your money is an acquired skill, and practice will bring progress.

3. ABILITY TO KEEP LIVING SPACES LIVABLE

Housecleaning (or for missionaries, apartment cleaning) can feel over-whelming. It's never really done. No matter how well you do it today, it has to be done again tomorrow. It's hard to stay ahead of the mess.

When my wife and I arrived in Ghana, many missionary apartments were poorly maintained. Dishes were unwashed. Food was left out. Dirty clothes were everywhere. Because of this, there were a lot of illnesses in the mission. In fact, on any given day we determined that about 15% of our missionaries were in their apartments rather than out proselyting because one or both missionaries were stuck in bed with stomach problems.

So we focused on doing something to improve the situation one task at a time. First, we bought microwave ovens for each apartment so mis-sionaries could prepare meals quickly and easily. Second, at every zone conference, we distributed recipes and presented cooking demonstrations. Third, we asked missionaries to make their beds every single day. It didn't take long before this was a standard embedded in our mission culture.

Admiral William McRaven, a former Navy SEAL, recently gave a commencement address at the University of Texas. In his speech, he emphasized that making your bed every day was not only expected in SEAL training but also became the basis for developing the habits and aptitudes to succeed as a SEAL. He stated that starting each day with this simple task creates a "can do" attitude that comes from a sense of accomplishment. Regardless of whatever else is occurring, making the bed is something each person can control. Each of us can do it to start the day off right, creating a little bit of order in a frequently disorderly world.

You can probably think of a lot of reasons not to make your bed, such as, "It's just going to get messed up again tonight," "I don't have time," "No one is going to see it anyway," "It's not important," or "My mother didn't make me. Why should I start now?"

Excuses are easy. But when it comes right down to it, so is making your bed. And that's the point: start each day by doing something easy. Just do it. Then regardless of whatever else happens that day, you've at least accomplished that one thing. In his book, *The Power of Habit,* Charles Duhigg says making your bed sets off a chain reaction that increases your likelihood of getting other things done during the day.[1] That's a pretty impressive result for just taking a couple of minutes to fix up some sheets and blankets!

Here's another endorsement for bed-making: Gretchen Rubin, author of *The Happiness Project* found through research that one of the most common, simple changes that led to happiness was making your bed each morning.[2] Wouldn't you take time to make your bed if you knew it would make you happier each day?

And it builds from there. Making your bed neat and tidy makes you want to make the room look neat and tidy, which consequently makes you want to make the rest of the apartment neat and tidy. More order means less chaos. Neatness and order create a subtle vibe of tranquility and competence. Competence because we know that we can do something that's completely in our control to start the day off right and tranquility because we are in a well kept and orderly setting.

Making your bed isn't the only thing you can do to make your living space livable, but it's a powerful first step. Get in the habit before your mission, and it will make a big difference in your attitude once you are in the mission field.

Another habit that doesn't take long and is easy to do is to clean the kitchen a little each day. Admiral McRaven puts it this way: "Want to change the world? Start by making your bed and washing the dishes . . . Now, you're in the driver's seat. Go out and make something happen."[3]

4. ABILITY TO EAT RIGHT AND STAY HEALTHY

If you're like most young men and young women preparing to enter the mission field, thus far you have left it up to others—mostly parents—to take care of meal planning and preparation. But if you get involved in buying food and cooking meals before your mission, you can experiment with what you like to cook, what you like to eat, and how to plan and prepare simple, nutritious meals. You'll develop skills you can use to serve others—like your companion—while on your mission.

You probably already know that eating junk foods or processed convenience foods too often can leave you feeling sluggish, while eating a balanced, nutritious diet can give you more energy and fuel for each day.

You can start right now to practice good eating habits that you can carry with you to the mission field.

Eating right doesn't mean you have to be a health food expert or become OCD (obsessive compulsive disorder) about organic foods. Like most things, it's about getting good information and staying balanced. But while there's lots of advice about healthy eating, when you get to the mission field it may be difficult to apply because food choices are limited, unavailable, overly expensive, or time consuming to prepare. Rather than thinking of eating healthy as an all-or-nothing proposition, try experimenting with different foods. Find healthy foods that are available and tasty, then simply use them more often. Eating a healthy, balanced diet will be much easier if you have already practiced doing it.

In addition to diet, exercise and personal hygiene are also important to staying healthy. One crucial yet often overlooked habit is taking care of your teeth and gums after eating. Proper dental hygiene, including brushing and flossing, can help to limit or eliminate harmful bacteria that can cause colds, flu, and other diseases. Getting proper rest and exercise, dressing appropriately for the weather, and washing your hands regularly also contribute to overall health.

These are simple tasks that are in your control that you can do every day to promote healthy habits. The legacy of the coronavirus pandemic is that simple things—including hand washing, disinfecting, eating, maintaining living spaces regularly, and consuming things that will boost your immune system—ward off both common and novel viruses that are all around us.

5. ABILITY TO GET FROM HERE TO THERE

As I mentioned previously, when I was a graduate teaching assistant, I worked with Stephen R. Covey, who became a well known author and consultant. He often said that while goal setting has many advocates, it has few well-founded principles. He decried the popular over-emphasis on end results without breaking down the required steps to arrive at those results. Create good processes, he said, and the results will then take care of themselves.

For instance, many times students set goals to get an "A" in a class. While this is admirable, he said, some of the end results of getting an "A" depend on a teacher's subjective evaluation or even test selection methods. Setting goals that others control could lead to frustration and disappointment.

He suggested that a better goal would be to focus on various processes for learning and performance, such as attending each class, reading all required material, and meeting with a tutor to understand difficult concepts. If well-defined and rigorously followed, such "process goals" are completely within our control. They are not just wishful thinking; they involve rigorous action. By following good processes, the end result of an "A" is more likely, and regardless of the outcome, is even more rewarding.

Understanding what leads to better results and setting rigorous process goals is the basis for the Japanese method of *kaizen*. Its focus is on continuous improvement, not just a "once and for all" leap into big dreams with misunderstood methods. Here is how *kaizen* can be applied to your daily routines to help you get more done each day now, and be more effective as a missionary later.

1. *Determine where your time and energy are wasted.* Take note of what you need to *stop* doing. What wastes your time? How much TV do you watch? What about video games? Or daydreaming? Or complaining about something that needs to be done, but not doing anything more than complaining? Make a list of these time wasters and work to shrink them into much smaller parts of your day.

2. *Ask yourself: what small steps can I take to be more productive or efficient?* Once you have reduced the number of time wasters, identify areas for improvement. The key here is to start with bite-sized changes. Think small. Often, our instinct is to go big. We get impatient and want results, if not overnight, then at least very quickly. Starting small may seem easy, but it takes great patience. If what you try doesn't improve things, try something else. Make the search for incremental improvement a new habit.

3. *Set aside time to review what's working and what could be improved.* When we get busy, we don't take time to evaluate what's working and what isn't. For *kaizen* to work, you need

to reflect on how things are going, especially when you sense a frictional point. Here are some questions to help your self-assessment:

- What was the "high point" of my day?
- What was the "low point" of my day?
- What does this tell me about my time wasters?
- What does this tell me about my areas for improvement?
- How do I reward myself for progress, not perfection?

These simple questions help us evaluate where we are spending our time and energy, and can help us set better goals or redirect the ones we have already established. Goal setting is about evaluating our progress and making adjustments, not just dreaming big and aspiring aimlessly. It takes practice and discipline to plan, do, and assess, but by doing so we are more likely to turn goals and dreams into accomplishments.

6. ABILITY TO DEAL WITH DISAPPOINTMENT

We all feel disappointment at times. Things don't always go the way we planned. But dealing with disappointment is not just a matter of getting used to being disappointed. When disappointments come our way, rather than letting them weigh us down, we need to learn from them.

Missionaries experience disappointment every day. Doors will be closed in your face, appointments will fall through, and investigators will decide not to continue with missionary discussions. Rejection is all around. While saying "when life gives you lemons, make lemonade" can be a start, developing resilience in the face of disappointment takes time, energy, and practice. Like other life skills, learning to handle rejection—and more importantly, not taking it personally when it comes—is worth developing before your mission so that you are not overwhelmed with it during your mission.

We often hear the phrase "go big or go home." In school, we learn that getting an "A" by scoring 90 percent or better is what we should hope for on exams. In reality, life is full of disappointments that impede our success. In many ways, achievements in life are more often like a baseball player's batting average. Anything over .300 is excellent! That means the batter is only getting a hit 30 percent of the time. Most of the time, he's getting out. But rather than letting this 70 percent rate of failure get him down, the batter keeps trying. Trying and learning is what keeps us going, helps us improve, and enables us to become our best.

Many of our feelings of disappointment may, in fact, come from inflated expectations. Dr. Dennis Greenberger in his research and clinical practice discovered that many mood disorders can be altered simply by changing expectations. "The secret to happiness is lowered expectations," he wrote in a *Mind Over Mood: Change How You Feel By Changing the Way You Think.*[4]

This is not to say we should have no expectations at all. Expectations motivate us to do many things. But self-help gurus and others may have missed the point when they tell us to "dream big." Few of us will be President or likely even a town mayor. Maybe it's less about dreaming big and more about making the most of what we have and who we are. In fact, in the eternal scheme of things, many activities that we might consider important don't really matter that much, and many others don't matter at all!

In his book *Happiness by Design: Finding Pleasure and Purpose in Everyday Life,* British psychologist Paul Dolan suggests that when we are disappointed we should look at the things that really make us happy and try to get more of them in our lives.[5] It's almost like he is saying: "Count your many blessings, name them one by one" (*Hymns,* no. 241). It seems it is the little things in life that make us happy, and reminding ourselves of that when we are disappointed will help us right our own ships or stabilize us when unexpected waves or events try to swamp us.

Young adults today feel even more stress and anxiety than their parents and other adults, according to a recent report from the American Psychological Association. The report says this is due to parental expectations, pressure to perform well in school, and comparisons they make on their own to others their same age.[6] They became disappointed not because they are incapable, but because they have received or created inflated expectations. "Go big or go home" may not be the best advice after all. Instead, seeing failed attempts as a part of growth may be a better perspective. Learning how to learn is much more important because it constantly keeps us looking forward, reaching out, and making progress on those everyday activities which build character and make us better people.

The truth is, the more we try, the more we will fail—but the more we will learn as well—and eventually, the more we will succeed. Life and missionary work are both about sustained effort over time.

7. ABILITY TO BUILD PERSONAL RELATIONSHIPS

We tend to develop friendships with others who have similar backgrounds and interests. However, missionaries are likely to meet or be assigned to be companions who come from very different backgrounds with very different interests. Your companion could come from another country or play sports or musical instruments you've never heard of, and you may have little in common other than your shared commitment to serve a mission. Sometimes these differences are hard to bridge. Since most missionaries have never had to learn how to relate to or live with someone different than themselves, this can be a huge challenge.

8. ABILITY TO DEVELOP A SERVICE MINDSET

Wards and stakes can help youth prepare for full-time missionary service by helping them to develop an orientation toward service. Such an orientation can help you become acquainted with people from different backgrounds and life experiences. The term "service learning" is being adopted at many universities and schools as an essential part of their curriculum. As a basic definition, here are service learning's three distinct components:

1. *Investigate*: What are we going to do and why is this important?
2. *Conduct*: What are the separate parts of the activity and how do we get results?
3. *De-Brief*: What did we learn from the activity about this situation and about ourselves?

In order to be effective as a missionary, you need to address similar questions. The goal is to find meaningful community engagement. It could be working with agencies that distribute food to the homeless, helping stage local events for the Special Olympics, or building low-cost homes with Habitat for Humanity. All of these are simple forms of community engagement. But through them, youth (who are potential missionaries) learn empathy. They don't just study scriptures on Sunday; they live the gospel all week long. The goal of community involvement is to develop Christlike attributes in a realistic setting. The learning that takes place can be enhanced by group discussions, and time for personal reflection.

A simple way of conducting an assessment following a service activity is to hand out index card to each person and ask them to write down their responses to these two questions:

1. What was the high point of the activity for you?
2. What was the low point of the activity for you?

Then, in small groups of three to five persons, have each person share their high and low points. Debriefing in this way keeps it simple, engages everyone, and combines the kind of activity-driven approach that often appeals to young men along with the personal sharing that often appeals to young women. What's important is that everyone learns together. Such service-learning activities provide a service orientation that is vital for a full-time missionary.

While doing service learning, it may be helpful to keep in mind that young men and young women tend to differ in the way they learn how to relate to each other. Researchers at the Stanford Children's Center say that girls often want to have long conversations about what's important, how things are going between them, and how they feel about it. Boys, on the other hand, tend to be less conversational. They develop or confirm relationships through shared experiences, sports, and activities rather than through personal sharing. As boys and girls reach adolescence, these tendencies continue, and last into adulthood.[7] Recognizing these differences in relating to others will also help missionaries in developing relationships with companions, investigators, and members.

9. ABILITY TO SET PERSONAL BOUNDARIES

Learning to set personal boundaries enables you to define yourself rather than letting others define who you are. Good people like and respect others who stand up for their beliefs—about the gospel and also about themselves. Teens often want to "go along to get along," and feel uncomfortable telling others about their standards. *For the Strength of Youth* guidelines can provide help in boundary setting by allowing youth to consciously choose to follow Church standards and by providing a text they can both study and share with others.

The truth is, everyone has different emotional needs which can vary over time and according to circumstances. Sometimes we act out of habit rather than considering both the needs of others and our own needs in a given situation. Observing and understanding others and what they may need, as well as taking responsibility for our own needs, builds both reliability and trust. It also facilitates the setting and respecting of personal boundaries and the personal boundaries of others. We all want to be treated with respect, and the more we respect others, the more likely we are to be respected.

Here's a "Red light/Green light" type of activity to consider in setting personal boundaries:

- ***Red light***: Stop comparing and competing so much with others. The more we look for the good in others and ourselves, the more we can train ourselves to see cooperation and not competition as the best way to develop friendships and relationships of trust.
- ***Green light***: Accept your own flaws. Once you do, no one can use them against you. And of course, recognizing them is also the first step in overcoming them.

- ***Red light***: Stop unrighteous judging. Snap judgments about others often turn out to be wrong once we get to know them.
- ***Green light***: Start emphasizing "random acts of kindness" in your daily life. "Cast your bread upon the waters, for after many days thou shalt find it again" (Ecclesiastes 11:1). Kindness produces even more kindness in return.

- ***Red light:*** Stop insisting on always being right. Avoid using absolutes like "always" and "never," which are usually associated with stereotypes. Don't insist on winning every argument. It puts others off because you seem to want to be the only judge in any conversation or interaction.

- ***Green light:*** Give others the benefit of the doubt. Sometimes we spend so much time pointing out others' mistakes that we fail to spend time enjoying their well-intended actions.[8]

10. ABILITY TO DEVELOP DAILY COPING SKILLS

We all have highs and lows in life. Some days may be filled with sunshine, others with rain. Planning ahead for rainy days helps us to make the most of them when they come. In Ghana, there is a distinct rainy season that lasts for months. During that season, it can rain eight to ten inches in less than a day, followed by eight to ten inches of rain the next day—and the day after that. So, as missionaries, we developed "rainy day plans" that helped us cope with the weather rather than merely sitting at home in our apartments. It was our way of choosing to use our time effectively, rather than let circumstances like the weather completely control us. We had a Plan B for many different types of circumstances.

Rainy day plans can help us in other aspects of our daily life as well. For instance, missionaries experience a lot of rejection. Every day. It comes almost as a guarantee to a missionary. More people are going to close their door on you than are going to open the door for you, regardless of where you serve. Handling rejection is never easy. No one likes it.

Even President Gordon B. Hinckley, when he was a full-time missionary, talked about his occasional discouragement because of the frequent rejection he felt while proselyting. He wrote to his father and said he felt he should no longer waste his time and his father's money. His father replied with a brief letter: "Dear Gordon, I have your recent letter. I have only one suggestion: forget yourself and go to work."[9]

There are two very distinct keys to coping with rejection:

1. **Don't take rejection personally—it says more about the other person than about you.**
2. **Doing something, especially physical activity, can improve your state of mind.**

But while saying "don't take rejection personally" is good advice, sometimes it's difficult *not* to take things personally. You may not make a sports or dance team. You may not win an award that you've worked hard to achieve. You may not get invited to a party, and it can seem like you are the only person left out. You may even feel like, in order to avoid getting hurt, that it's not worth it to ever try again.

It's okay to acknowledge these hurt feelings. But it's not healthy to continue to wallow in them. Give them their due, for a few hours or a few days. Then deliberately decide to move on. There is nothing like moving forward to help us leave the past behind. When pioneers in southern Utah first arrived, they started building dams to provide irrigation water for the crops they planted. In St. George, however, those dams were washed out by flash floods—again and again, year after year, despite faithful prayers amid desperate conditions. But the pioneers in St. George neither blamed God nor gave up hope. Instead they rebuilt and continued trying. Time after time they rebuilt washed out dams and flooded irrigation ditches. They forgot about themselves, went to work, and never gave up hope. Today, the city of St. George stands as a monument to their perseverance.

The scriptures are filled with messages of hope, for the here and now as well as for the eternities. Hope is compelling and can give us a sense of purpose even when we are down or discouraged. We read in Psalms, "The Lord taketh pleasure . . . in those that hope in his mercy" (147:11).

Young adults who have already learned to "forget [themselves] and go to work" are already well prepared for the mission field.

SUMMARY

These life skills can, of course, be learned while serving a mission. But if they are developed prior to missionary service then they will make the transition into missionary life easier and more complete. Church leaders have stressed the importance of being prepared when arriving in the mission field. Attending seminary, participating in family scripture study, and daily personal prayer are, of course, important aspects of this preparation. They are necessary but not sufficient. Acquiring the life skills described in this chapter are also important ingredients for arriving at the mission field prepared and ready to go. The more each potential missionary makes a conscious effort to develop these skills ahead of time, the more each of them will be able to be effective, beginning with the day they arrive in the mission field.

REFERENCES

1. Charles Duhigg, *The Power of Habit* (New York: Random House, 2014), p. 546.
2. Gretchen Rubin, *The Happiness Project* (New York: Harper, 2009).
3. William H. McRaven, *Make Your Bed: Small Things That Can Change Your Life and Maybe the World* (New York: Grand Central Publishing, 2017).
4. Dennis Greenberger and Christine A. Padesky, *Mind Over Mood: Changing How You Feel By Changing How You Think* (New York: Guilford Press, 1996).
5. Paul Dolan, *Happiness By Design: Change What You Do, Not How You Think* (New York: Penguin, 2014).
6. American Psychological Association, *Stress in America: Are Teens Adopting Adults Stress Habits* (Washington, D.C. APA, 2014), 12.
7. "Default—Stanford Children's Health." Stanford Children's Health—Lucile Packard Children's Hospital Stanford.
8. Adapted from "Red Light/Green Light: Setting Clear Boundaries," CourageCompasstherapy.com.
9. Sheri L. Dew, "The 2 Sentences That Changed President Gordon B. Hinckley's Life Forever," *LDS Living*, May 16, 2017, ldsliving.com/The-2-Sentences-That-Changed-President-Gordon-B-Hinckley-s-Life-Forever/s/85398.

Chapter 3

WHAT IT TAKES

Competencies and self-directed learning

Regardless of our age, we all like to sing the Primary song:

> I hope they call me on a mission
> When I have grown a foot or two.
> I hope by then I will be ready
> To teach and preach and work as missionaries do.
> (*Children's Songbook*, 169)

But what do missionaries actually do each day, and how can they prepare and be ready once they arrive in the mission field?

When I asked hundreds of new missionaries this question over the years as they came either to the Texas Houston Mission or to the Ghana Accra West Mission, the most frequent answer was "prepare by reading *Preach My Gospel*." Good advice. There are tons of tips and suggestions in *Preach My Gospel*. So many suggestions, in fact, that it is easy to get overwhelmed by them and overlook some of the themes, patterns, skills, and abilities—key competencies—that *Preach My Gospel* prescribes for missionaries.

COMPETENCIES

Competencies is a common term used in business and other organizations today to describe knowledge, skills, and abilities along with effective methods and best practices in getting things done in a task or for an assignment. Competencies are often broken down into ability levels such as basic, intermediate, and expert. You acquire basic competencies as you watch and observe, read, and study, and practice and improve.

However, to become truly *expert* you will need to make a concerted effort not only to understand skills identified in *Preach My Gospel* but to fully master them. Some missionaries never fully grasp required competencies, while others remain at a basic level for their entire missions. However, if you take the time to understand fully key competencies in *Preach My Gospel*, and steadily improve your ability, you will develop your own *personal presence* that will enable you to have experiences that others only wish they could have.

Competencies may not be a familiar term to you so let's look at some examples to better understand what they are, and how you can use them to improve your ability to share the gospel. It's easy to see how competencies work in sports. Baseball, for instance, has hitting, throwing, catching, and running of bases. Players learn fundamentals from playing with friends and family for fun, and competing in leagues at a young age. In addition to the fundamentals, as they progress, players learn how to improve their skill level and add to their repertoire. For instance, hitting involves more than merely making contact with the ball. It also includes bunting, making contact for a sacrifice fly ball, executing squeeze plays, delivering hit and run plays, and other degrees of difficulty that, if performed well, make an athlete a complete and well-rounded ball player.

Missionary work is similar. There are various competencies—knowledge and skill requirements—as well as ability levels in sharing the gospel for you to learn and later master. You might come by some of these competencies intuitively, but most of them will require practice, effort, observation, feedback, and consistent improvement.

In closely examining *Preach My Gospel*, the Church has included fifty-two separate and distinct missionary competencies in that resource guidebook. "What?" you may be saying. "Are you kidding? There are 52 competencies in *Preach My Gospel*?" Yep, there are fifty-two of them. I know, that's a lot! But you don't have to learn them all at once, and some of them you may have already. There's an old saying "by the yard, it's hard; by the inch, it's a cinch." So yes, there are fifty-two competencies, but they aren't learned all at once. They are mastered one at a time. Learning to be a good missionary takes time and practice along with coaching and personal assessment—just like learning how to do anything else. It's more than simply accepting a call and suddenly being proficient. As you strive to faithfully develop these competencies, the Holy Ghost will help you. Step by step, you will improve as you call down the powers of Heaven to help you.

"For behold, thus saith the Lord God: I will give unto the children of men line upon line, precept upon precept, here a little and there a little; and blessed are those who hearken unto my precepts, and lend an ear unto my counsel, for they shall learn wisdom; for unto him that receiveth I will give more; and from them that shall say, We have enough, from them shall be taken away even that which they have" (2 Nephi 28:30).

GETTING STARTED

So, let's get started. Now that you've "grown a foot or two" from Primary days, what does it take to be an effective missionary? As I said there are fifty-two competencies embedded in *Preach My Gospel*. I didn't make up a single one of them. I just identified them. Extracting competencies is something that I did when I worked for ExxonMobil—at the time, the most profitable company in the world. Bigger than Walmart or Apple or Amazon in its day. My job was to look at competencies required for certain jobs, break down their components, and develop training programs to help people succeed in them. So, when I was called as a mission president, I did the same thing with *Preach My Gospel*. I looked at the competencies: knowledge, skills, and abilities—which are included in *Preach My Gospel* and simply listed them. Perhaps like you, I was surprised to discover there were so many of them. I didn't think there would be so many. Initially it seemed overwhelming to try to help missionaries acquire them.

As I studied and prayed and tried to work out an approach that would help missionaries, a bolt of inspiration came. I put every one of those fifty-two competencies on a deck of cards. Each card contained just one competency. Then, I asked the entire mission to rank the ones that mattered most. The ones that any good missionary must learn how to do to become effective. Eventually, we eliminated twenty-two of them. Fifty-two is too many anyway, and some were not used often, so we slimmed down *Preach My Gospel's* list to a Top 30. This is a more manageable number of skills that we could work on developing. We could focus on getting better at what we were actually called to do.

As Benjamin Franklin once said: "Without continual growth and progress, such words as improvement, success, and achievement have no meaning." I've sent this Top 30 list to other mission presidents—more than a dozen have used them with missionaries just like you. I've also discussed this list of competencies with many other missionaries and mission presidents—many have used them with missionaries just like you.

FOUNDATIONAL MISSIONARY COMPETENCIES

Let's get started then. First, here's a list of the seven foundational competencies on which the others are built. Let's start with these.

1. Understanding local priesthood leaders' perspectives
2. Obeying the commandments and mission rules with exactness
3. Focusing on commitments and baptismal interview questions in teaching
4. Recording spiritual impressions in appropriate places
5. Concerning myself with my own personal progress rather than my progress compared to others
6. Describing persuasively my thoughts and feelings about the Book of Mormon to others
7. Visualizing the people I teach kneeling at the altar in the temple

These foundational missionary competencies—once well established—form the basis for which other competencies can then be refined and polished. Like the foundation of a house, developing these competencies first enables you to build upon a stable basis and add additional features as you grow. Without these foundational competencies, none of the other competencies matter.

Describing competencies from *Preach My Gospel* is easy; developing them takes patience and practice, just like developing any other skill. These Top 30 competencies from *Preach My Gospel* apply to all missionaries, but details on how best to acquire them and use them will vary by mission and local circumstances.

Here is an illustration of how you might evaluate your skill level with the foundational competencies.

For example, "Describe persuasively your thoughts and feelings about the Book of Mormon" is an essential competency. If you can tell important stories from it and relate appropriate passages from the Book of Mormon to daily life, then you are on your way. If you can ask inspired questions that enable investigators to share their own thoughts and feelings about the Book of Mormon, then you are really progressing. If you can help investigators see for themselves the truths of the gospel, and invite the Spirit so powerfully that the Holy Ghost confirms the witness you give about the truths of the Book of Mormon, you are serving as disciples of old. In developing each competency, strive simply to improve and to set goals to get better, not simply to evaluate your ability. **Focus on progress, not perfection.** Strive to invite the Spirit by becoming better at each competency. "Wherefore, he that preacheth and he that receiveth, understand one another, and both are edified and rejoice together" (Doctrine and Covenants 50:22).

Mastering a competency is more than a simple mechanical process of analyzing and deliberating about what it. The Holy Ghost must guide you in your learning process. As Commissioner of the Church Educational System Elder Kim B. Clark said,

I know that learning is not easy. You know that too! Life in mortality and the natural man and woman in all of us makes it hard to keep learning. It is hard to stay open to new ideas and new ways of working. Sometimes the Lord's plan for stretching us and challenging us is hard. It can be hard to remain ready to repent, and grow, and change according to our Father's plan. In the face of these difficulties, it is not surprising that we sometimes think,

"There's no way I can do this." But by sticking with it, we can grow in unexpected ways.

"If you really desire to learn deeply, if your hearts and your mind are open to learning, and if you act on that desire, the Lord will bless you. When you do your part—pray in faith, prepare, study, engage actively, and do your very best—the Holy Ghost will teach you to magnify your capacity to act on what you learn, and help you become what the Lord wants you to become."[1]

Read these examples from the scriptures of the gifts and blessings that come through the ministry of the Holy Ghost:

- Teaches all things (John 14:26)
- Guides us into all truth (John 16:13)
- Shows all things we should do (Luke 12:12)
- Fills us with wisdom and understanding (D&C 46:11–26)
- Fills us with power (Acts 1:8)
- Gives us such gifts as wisdom, knowledge, faith, discernment (1 Corinthians 12:8–12)
- Helps with our infirmities (Romans 8:26)
- Intercedes so we know what to pray for (Romans 8:26)
- Enables us to abide in hope (Romans 15:13)
- Snctifies us (3 Nephi 27:20)

Understanding, learning, and applying competencies may be a "new way of learning" for many missionaries, but you can do it! You can grow and learn to do things differently, and reap the blessings that come with improvement. As Doctrine and Covenants 82:18 reminds us, "and all this for the benefit of the church of the living God, that every man may improve upon his talent, that every man may gain other talents, yea, even an hundred fold."

WHY COMPETENCIES

An important consideration in developing missionary knowledge, skills, and abilities—competencies—is to answer the *why* questions. Why do you want to get better? To show off to someone else? Get praised by the mission president? Talk potential investigators into getting baptized? None of these are good reasons and likely will spoil your efforts to improve. But you must also go beyond the vague reasons like "because I want to serve better and achieve my potential." Such vague, well-meaning objectives are neither compelling nor specific enough to be motivational. Dig deeper. Consider your purpose as a missionary. Elder Dieter F. Uchtdorf suggested some reasons for improvement in missionary service, which I have paraphrased and expanded as follows:

- Come, add your strengths to ours.
- Become better and happier by drawing closer to the Lord.
- Receive saving ordinances and help others receive them as well.
- Build and strengthen a culture of healing, kindness, and mercy.[2]

So, how do you begin? By assessing yourself. No one knows better than you do about how well you are performing or what you need to do to improve. No test, no measurement, no examination will be as effective as your own self-assessment. After all, no one knows you as well as you do! Malcom Knowles (a pioneer in adult development) maintains that we learn and grow best when we examine our own experiences, and make personal decisions to improve. Rather than relying on formal classroom settings, we learn best informally through observation, feedback, self-reflection, and personal goal setting. This more informal, more personal method of development and growth is called "self-directed learning."

SELF-DIRECTED LEARNING

There are three primary reasons for self-directed learning. First, there is convincing evidence that when we take the initiative in learning (as proactive learners) that we learn more, and learn better than those who sit passively waiting to be taught (as reactive learners). You learn more purposefully and with greater motivation when you observe, assess, and improve on your own.

A second reason for self-directed learning is that it enhances your ability to take responsibility for your own life—to be in the driver's seat controlling how you want to direct yourself, and what matters most to you.

Lastly, self-directed learning empowers you to deal more positively with anxiety, frustration, and failure. Thus, we learn from past experience rather than merely becoming weighed down by difficulties.

In an *Ensign* article titled "Making Your Life a Soul Stirring Journey of Personal Growth," Elder Jeffrey R. Holland wrote:

> You can see that the kind of learning I'm talking about is far too big to fit into a classroom or to be wrapped up in a 50-minute lesson. Scriptures, prophets, parents, sunshine, rainy days, spiritual promptings, and the everyday curriculum of life itself all provide opportunities for us to learn about God and His plan, for surely "all things bear record" of Him (Moses 6:63). Eventually we all discover that He is willing to teach us not only at church but anywhere and anytime—in informal moments with our children and our friends, our neighbor or our workmates, the man or woman we see on the bus or the employee who helps us at the market—wherever and whenever we are willing to learn.[3]

This kind of informal learning, as Elder Holland notes, can take place anywhere and is derived from our own experience. Competencies in missionary work give us some guidance, but ultimately our own personal assessment provides the needed direction. This type of self-directed learning leaves every missionary in control of both assessment and development.

GETTING STARTED

So how does it work? Here's what happened in the Ghana Accra West Mission and what is occurring elsewhere around the world which you can do on your own:

1. Make a card deck with each of the seven (7) foundational missionary competencies and the twenty-three (23) supporting competencies on an individual card so that you have a deck of cards with one competency on each card. Here is the entire list of missionary competencies and how your own card deck should look:

SEVEN FOUNDATIONAL COMPETENCIES

Understanding local priesthood leaders' perspectives

Obeying the commandments and mission rules with exactness

Focusing on commitments and baptismal interview questions in teaching

Describing persuasively my thoughts and feelings about the Book of Mormon to others

Recording spiritual impressions in appropriate places

Concerning myself with my own personal progress rather than my progress compared to others

Visualizing people I teach kneeling at the altar of the temple

23 SUPPORTING COMPETENCIES

Serving and doing good regardless of whether people accept our message

Loving the people that I teach, and ensuring that I desire only their salvation

Treasuring up continually the doctrines of the gospel of Jesus Christ

Discerning people's unspoken questions or concerns

Expressing gratitude diligently to the Lord and others

Staying on the lookout for new people to teach throughout the day

Explaining how and why I know a gospel principle is true so others can also gain this knowledge	Refraining from thinking I am better than others whose traditions or background are different than my own	Explaining "key definitions" in each lesson
Setting goals regularly to become a more effective missionary	Conducting daily and weekly companionship planning sessions	Resisting becoming critical of my companion or others, especially when impatient
Aniticipating and preparing in advance to address questions before each appointment	Conveying knowledgeably and profoundly my testimony of the First Vision	Striving to find and teach families who support each other in living the gospel
Studying the scriptures effectively each day	Teaching and helping people express the feelings of their heart in prayer	Recognizing the Lord is pleased with my best efforts, even when I experience disappointment
Making regular entries into the Area Book	Using "Questions to Ask after You Teach" regularly to build trust and resolve concerns	Discussing traditional beliefs, which may not be consistent with gospel principles, with people
Refining and modifying lesson plans to meet the needs of those I teach	Evaluating each teaching appointment with my companion when it is complete	

2. Now, sort through the card deck assessing your own competencies. Use the three different categories below to help you decide what is most important for you to work on right now. To begin with, put ten cards in each category so that you have an equal number of cards in "Strengths," "Don't Know," and "Needs Improvement."

Strengths	Don't Know	Needs Improvement

3. Following this initial sifting, pick out your top three "Strengths" cards and at the same time identify your three most significant personal gaps in "Needs Improvement." This gives you a "critical few" competencies to focus on right now! You must identify your strengths so that you can share with others as well as rely upon them yourself when times are hard or when things seem difficult. Don't underestimate your strengths or ignore them. It's just as important to acknowledge your strengths as it is to identify areas that need improvement. Include both in your personal planning.

4. Rely on your strengths—we all have them. You can then turn something you are good at into a skill or ability that is even better. Think "good, better, best." Become a role model for others in that skill or ability area. Acknowledge it, use it, and share it.

5. Set goals to improve in the three areas for improvement you identified as well. Read more about this competency in *Preach My Gospel*. Ask others about it. Study prophets in the scriptures and use the Topical Guide to help you discover more ways to improve. Ask for suggestions from your companion, friends, family members, and local leaders.

6. Most of all recognize its progress, not perfection, which matters most. Keep at it. Become a lifelong learner. The race is not to the swiftest, but to the person who endures to the end.

Using this structured approach has at least five benefits:

1. It provides a way for you to identify your own strengths and needs-improvement areas, thereby increasing personal ownership.

2. It gives you a way to interact with others on skill gaps you've identified and so you can ask for help in specific areas.

3. It reinforces competencies—or skills and abilities—embedded in *Preach My Gospel* and avoids creating a separate program or alternative approach.
4. It gives you a way to develop leadership skills, so you can help your companion and other missionaries.
5. It reinforces lifelong learning outcomes emphasized in the Church manual *Teaching in the Savior's Way*.

HOW TO ASSESS YOURSELF

As human beings it can be difficult to accurately appraise our strengths and improvement areas. You may have inflated views of some of your strengths, or you may be overly critical about things you need to improve. A mission is an opportunity to learn skills in self-assessment along with other life skills. It may take some time and effort to overcome inertia and get going, but as the old saying goes, "there's no time like the present to get started."

As you push yourself, work against the tendency to feel discouraged or to feel that improvement is hopeless. Recognizing your strengths helps with that. Don't gloss over or dismiss your strengths. Recognizing them not only fortifies you against discouragement but also allows you to build on those things you do really well and get even better at them.

The trick is to assess your missionary competencies honestly—but not rate your inherent worthiness as a missionary. You are called of the Lord, and He will help you succeed.

Elder Jeffrey R. Holland has said:

As children of God, we should not demean or vilify ourselves, as if beating up on ourselves is somehow going to make us the person God wants us to become. No! With a willingness to repent and a desire for increased righteousness always in our hearts, I would hope we could pursue personal improvement in a way that doesn't include getting ulcers or anorexia, feeling depressed or demolishing our self-esteem. That is *not* what the Lord wants for

Primary children or anyone else who honestly sings, "I'm trying to be like Jesus."[4]

Look upon self-appraisal as identifying a new path for yourself and persistently walking down it. Sometimes this may require abandoning old habits and acquiring new ones.

Experts describe relearning, or changing habitual emotions and behavior, as similar to retraining a horse that is used to taking a familiar route. If you ride a horse on the same path every time, he will only reluctantly go down a new path. Every time the horse gets to a particular juncture, he will hesitate. It's only with consistently guiding the horse down the new path that he will unlearn the old route, and relearn the new one. As futurist Alvin Toffler once wrote: "The illiterate of the 21st century will not be those who cannot read or write, but those who cannot learn, unlearn, and relearn."

A good example might be the way missionaries were forced to proselyte during the coronavirus pandemic. Confined to their apartments, traditional ways of contacting by knocking on doors and in-person teaching had to be replaced by virtual contacting and remote teaching. This required missionaries to "unlearn" old ways of doing things and replace them with new ways of performing missionary service.

A self-assessment is not a test; it's an honest appraisal of strengths and areas in need of improvement. It's more of an art than a science which simply means there's no right or wrong way to do it, and the more you do it the better you will get.

When the Prophet Joseph emerged from the Sacred Grove and returned home, his mother noticed that he was pensive and asked him if he was well. He replied that he was not ill and then said these remarkable five words: "I have learned for myself" (Joseph Smith—History 1:20). Through his curiosity, his willingness to act, and through his own experience, the Prophet *learned for himself*. In the same way, you can learn for yourself how to become a better missionary.

DEVELOPING A SELF-DIRECTED LEARNING PLAN

We read in Doctrine and Covenants 88:118 that we must learn "by study and also by faith." Sometimes we must experiment not only with the word to plant in our hearts (Alma 32), but also experiment with ways to improve our teaching, our relationships, and our ministry. Paul wrote that "by the experiment of this ministry they glorify God" (2 Corinthians 9:13). In other words, our Heavenly Father is pleased when we constantly strive to improve even when we make mistakes or fall short of our goals. In striving, in trying, and in experimenting we improve.

The best self-directed learning plans are simple, direct, and focus on a "growth mindset." This term, coined by Stanford University Professor Carol Dweck in her book *Mindset: Changing the Way You Think To Fulfill Your Potential,* shows that people with a *fixed mindset* assume that they're born with a particular set of skills that they can't change. However, people with a *growth mindset* believe that intelligence and talent are just the starting point, and that success comes through attitude, effort, and continuous learning.[5]

A personal learning plan has the following components (adapted from *Preach My Gospel* "Developing Christlike Attributes"). Use this clear, step-by-step approach to create your own personal development plan:

1. A clear and specific description of what you want to improve upon or do better
    * Can you visualize it?
    * Can you list its characteristics and attributes?
2. A written outline of how you are going to achieve this
    * Writing creates focus and accountability
    * Inspiration often comes as we write our thoughts and feelings
3. Questions you will ask yourself along the way to help you
    * The word "seek" is used more than five hundred times in the scriptures. Asking questions is the best way to "seek" answers.
    * The best questions are action-oriented and begin with "what" or "how."

4. Ways you will involve the Lord through prayer, and your companion and mission president through discussion
    - Inspiration comes as we seek it. "Pray always, and I will pour out my spirit upon you, and great shall be your blessing" (Doctrine and Covenants 19:38).
    - "Every purpose is established by counsel" (Proverbs 20:18).
5. How you will measure your progress through achievements or reaching a certain milestone
6. A target, deadline, or schedule to help you stay focused

SUMMARY

Since these competencies are derived from *Preach My Gospel*, they give you a clear set of skills and abilities to develop regardless of where you serve. When you break down and unpack what it takes to successfully meet the demands of missionary life, these competencies give you both a clear direction and a yardstick for assessing how well you are doing. Just as athletes and musicians are always looking for ways to develop the finer points of their crafts, you can do the same by continually using these competencies to assess and improve your own contributions to move the Lord's work forward.

REFERENCES

1. Kim B. Clark, "Learning for the Whole Soul," *Ensign*, August 2017, 23.
2. Dieter F. Uchtdorf, "Believe, Love, Do," *Ensign,* October 2018.
3. Jeffrey R. Holland, "Making Your Life a Soul-Stirring Journey of Personal Growth," *Ensign*, December 2018.
4. Jeffrey R. Holland, "Be Ye Therefore Perfect—Eventually," *Ensign,* November 2017.
5. Carol Dweck, *Mindset: Changing the Way You Think to Fulfill Your Potential* (Boston: Little, Brown, 2017).

Chapter 4

HOW TO MAKE THE MOST
OF STUDY TIME

Interactive gospel study

Preach My Gospel notes that "Many missionaries struggle to know how to study effectively" (17). It is true, this is a very common problem. We go to school, are given assignments to read, and typically take a quiz or write a paper with structured answers to structured questions to test our knowledge. But teaching the gospel requires much more than simply memorizing a few scriptures and then repeating them aloud occasionally to investigators.

Getting good results from your study depends on four key attributes:

1. Having a strong desire to learn
2. Studying with real intent
3. Hungering and thirsting after righteousness
4. Searching for answers to the questions and concerns of those you are teaching

In addition to these four attributes and certainly make a difference in effective study, there is much to be gained by also looking at how, when, and where to study. We often cite D&C 88:118 which tells us to "seek learning, even by study and also by faith," but the first part of that scripture, which is cited less often, is also important: "And as all have not faith, *seek ye diligently* and *teach one another* words of wisdom" (emphasis added). Such diligent and interactive study and learning is not limited to a classroom but can be the basis for personal and companion study.

The goal of gospel learning is not merely to be well versed, but instead to continually *seek diligently*. There is something to be said for continuing to learn, grow, and improve. We learn in many different ways: through study, through faith, through life experiences, through each other, through meditation, through inspiration, and even line upon line. In *Mere Christianity*, C. S. Lewis wrote, "God is no fonder of intellectual slackers than He is of any other slacker." It is the idle mind that is the Devil's workshop. An active mind is continually learning, developing, and progressing.

One of the best ways to learn is to use as many physical senses as possible to see, hear, touch, recite, associate, and reflect when studying. Instead of just reading a talk or scripture verses, try describing what you've read to a friend, or maybe take notes about a discussion, share those notes later with others, think about them and make connections to other life experiences you've had. As you go throughout the day, reword those thoughts so that you "own the message" and can give a fresh and original perspective on it. By learning in more than one way, you are further solidifying new insights in your mind.

Here are six important ways to learn the gospel better so that you can teach it more effectively:

1. SEEK

As previously mentioned, the word *seek* is used over five hundred times in the scriptures, so it must be quite important. Beyond the number of times it is used in the scriptures, it is often emphasized in general conference talks and many other religious settings. The Prophet Joseph Smith told us that the gospel is so broad and deep that only by diligently seeking the Savior can we grasp its full significance:

A fanciful and flowery and heated imagination beware of; because the things of God are of deep import; and time, and experience, and careful and ponderous and solemn thoughts can only find them out. Thy mind, O man! if thou wilt lead a soul unto salvation, must stretch as high as the utmost heavens, and search into and contemplate the darkest abyss, and the broad expanse of eternity—thou must commune with God.[1]

Seeking and studying with real intent can occur through personal study, companion study, district study, as well as by reading the scriptures chronologically or topically. When you study the gospel by topic with your companion or district, the material opens doors for fellowship and discussion. When two or more missionaries are sharing not only what they've read but also what it means to them, they are able to do more than just increase their gospel knowledge, they are able to draw closer to each other. A group of missionaries facing similar situations are in a unique position to "counsel together" and to "take counsel from one another" because they already have some common ground for discussion—they are coexisting with a shared purpose.

Here's one way to have an ongoing topical study of the gospel either individually, with your companion, or with others:

- Look up every parallel and relative scriptural passage on the subject you are studying. There will be primary references and secondary references. Find out about the context of particular verses. Use a systematic way to gather and sort information. Create topical categories or "bins" to put different points of view or people's reactions from the scriptures themselves to what is said.
- Use the Bible Dictionary, the Topical Guide, and perhaps a concordance to ensure the scriptural words you are reading mean the same thing in different contexts. Many words have multiple meanings. Use the footnotes to look up other parallel passages.
- Look up any contrasting scriptural passages. Look for qualifying statements that are definitive.
- See if there are clarifications to the doctrine from modern revelation through general conference addresses. When sorting through different scriptural passages, determine which passages are clear and which are unclear, which are relevant, and which are less applicable.

    Additionally, putting things into our own words enhances recall and allows us to apply scripture verses when teaching.

- Write in your own words the meaning of difficult passages. Don't simply paraphrase or copy what others have said. Write how you understand a passage or series of passages.
- Find ways to apply what you have learned. Everything can be applied to us today. Elder Neal A. Maxwell of the Quorum of the Twelve Apostles said: "May we then do . . . what Nephi did when studying the scriptures, namely, to 'liken all scriptures' unto ourselves (1 Nephi 19:23). This is something that doesn't happen often enough in the Church. We read the scriptures, but often we do not 'liken' them."[2]

2. PONDER

"For my soul delighteth in the scriptures and my heart pondereth them . . . Behold, my soul delighteth in the things of the Lord; and my heart pondereth continually upon the things which I have seen and heard" (2 Nephi 4:15–16).

"The mind is sharper and keener in seclusion and uninterrupted solitude," wrote inventor Nikola Tesla. "Originality thrives in seclusion free of outside influences beating upon us to cripple the creative mind. Be alone— that is the secret of invention: be alone, that is when ideas are born."

Pondering is not a passive process. It is active and full of emotional involvement. Pondering is the conscious effort of trying to understand something that is alluded to you. It is the act of pulling pieces of information from all over the landscape of your understanding and trying to make something new out of it. This is why pondering works so well with gospel topics; it is a prime way to set yourself up for inspiration and revelation from the Holy Ghost. Always pray for guidance and help in your pondering, and invite the Spirit when seeking revelation.

Pondering is always purposeful. It is not daydreaming or abstract or fanciful thinking. President David O. McKay said that pondering or meditation is "deep, continued reflection on some religious theme . . . through which we pass into the presence of the Lord."[3] Such pondering can occur as we reflect on messages from our gospel study. In the Church's booklet *Adjusting to Missionary Life,* there are various examples given of ways we can ponder when discouraged and uncertain or when perfectionism intrudes, and we feel inadequate for the tasks at hand.

From the booklet, here are three specific examples of how we can use pondering to adjust our mindset and feel the confirming influence of the Holy Ghost when discouraged or uncertain:

- **Talk back to negative thinking.** Right now, or before bed tonight, list your negative thoughts from today on paper; then rewrite them to be more hopeful, truthful, and encouraging.
- **Be kind to yourself.** Talk to yourself with the same kind, comforting words you would use with someone else [when empathizing]. Everyone gets frustrated or makes mistakes sometimes. Know that the Lord understands. Imagine Him sitting close to you, listening, and offering support. Remember, thoughts of helplessness, hopelessness, or harsh condemnation are not from the Lord.
- **Refocus on gratitude.** Take note of what is around you. Focus for a few minutes on what is right, good, and positive about yourself and the world [or your circumstances]. Offer a prayer of gratitude for at least five specific things.

3. DISCOVER

Paul occasionally used the metaphor of a race and said that it is important to run it well. While perhaps a good message, nowhere do the scriptures say, "the race is not to the swift but the one who endures to the end." This is a modern saying. We often conflate or combine messages from different sources and are surprised when we cannot find what we are looking for in the scriptures.

In Ecclesiastes, the Preacher said, "I returned, and saw under the sun, that the race is not to the swift nor the battle to the strong, neither yet bread to the wise, nor yet riches to men of understanding, nor yet favour to men of skill; but time and chance happeneth to them all" (Ecclesiastes 9:11).

This scripture refers to the vagaries of life more than enduring to the end; it's a helpful message but not the same message as the conflated saying we often quote.

Other conflated sayings or references can lead us even more astray. A close reading of the scriptures themselves both enriches our understanding and reminds us that "no prophecy of the scripture is of any private interpretation" (2 Peter 1:20).

Another frequently cited and conflated scripture occurs in Luke 10:38–42. Jesus was traveling. He entered a village and went to Martha's house. Verse 39 says that Martha had a sister whose name was Mary, and when the Savior was there "Mary, which also sat at Jesus' feet . . . heard his word."

Many have mistakenly assumed that Mary sat at Jesus' feet alone while Martha worked in the kitchen. Not so. Luke carefully explains that they both sat there to hear the words of eternal life. Luke then records that "Martha was cumbered about "much serving."

Often, we assume this serving was working in the kitchen or preparing a meal. However, the same word translated here as "serving" is also used in Acts 6:1–6, and scholars say it is associated with church service and ministry—not table service or food preparation at all. More likely, Martha was cumbered with church service rather than gospel living, and the Savior was redirecting her toward eternal ideals, more than numbers and reports. The domestic interpretation of the term "serving" was popularized by Clement and Origen in the Third century along with the distinction between "contemplative life" and practical activities, scholars note. It is not part of Luke's account.

Lastly, we tend to recall that the Savior said to Martha that Mary had chosen the *better part* and that Martha should follow suit. However, verse 42 says: "But one thing is needful: and Mary hath chosen that good part." Mary has chosen that *good part*—there is no comparison in the Savior's words between Mary's part and Martha's part. Both are necessary. The Savior tells Martha, however, not to be burdened with her part, not to be cumbered or stressed about her part.[4]

In addition to avoiding conflating the scriptures and instead reading them closely, we can also seek inspiration as we study. Such inspiration often comes as the first spiritual impression we receive while studying. The Prophet Joseph Smith said:

> A person may profit by noticing the first intimation of the spirit of revelation; for instance, when you feel pure intelligence flowing into you, it may give you sudden strokes of ideas, so that by noticing it, you may find it fulfilled the same day or soon; (i.e.) those things that were presented unto your minds by the Spirit of God, will come to pass; and thus by learning the Spirit of God and understanding it, you may grow into the principle of revelation, until you become perfect in Christ Jesus.[5]

Such spiritual impressions are available to all of us. Modern day prophets have told us over and over again that the Lord is more inclined to give us spiritual impressions and personal revelation than we are ready to receive. He is ready, while we may not be. How does this happen? Elder Patrick Kearon of the Seventy noted, "We may not *know* we are doing it, but occasionally we cut ourselves off from divine communication. . . . When we stay up too late and work too hard in order to meet our daily demands, fatigue sets in, we become overtired, and the world looks like a much gloomier place; things get out of perspective and out of proportion."[6]

Practical matters enhance or interfere with our spiritual bearings. For good reason, the *Missionary Standards for Disciples of Jesus Christ* includes sufficient rest, eating well, and exercising (see 4.1–4.3). Such ordinary activities are as necessary as study, prayer, and service to our spiritual well-being.

4. TRANSFORM

Tad Callister, former Sunday School General President, said that our purpose in learning the gospel is not just to become more knowledgeable, but to become more converted. It is about transforming our lives for the better. It can be painful to go through a transformation of some of our deeply held beliefs, and experience a deeper discovery of ourselves. Joseph Campbell, the author of *The Hero with a Thousand Faces,* maintains that developing strong inner convictions is a fragile process. He also says that we do it best when we identify with personal heroes, and find ways to develop the same courage and integrity they have when life tests our mettle.[7] "What would Nephi or Captain Moroni or the Savior do here?" Implicit in this assessment is that integrity and individuality is an emotionally and psychologically difficult process. On the path to glory, heroes always face demons—both inside and outside themselves.

As we overthrow old ways of thinking and reach deeper into ourselves, we become more open. We are simultaneously discovering and incubating our inner spiritual hero. This brings out all sorts of insecurities and confusions, but it also brings out triumphs.

Elder David A. Bednar noted:

The essence of the gospel of Jesus Christ entails a fundamental and permanent change in our very nature made possible through the Savior's Atonement. True conversion brings a change in one's beliefs, heart, and life to accept and conform to the will of God (see Acts 3:19; 3 Nephi 9:20) and includes a conscious commitment to become a disciple of Christ.[8]

Here is a series of steps that can help us make the spiritual transformation that our Heavenly Father wants us to make in becoming like Him:

1. Make a list of reasons why you want to make certain changes. Write down all the great things that will happen once your transformation is complete. This will motivate you when you're tempted to fall back into your old habits.

2. Conversion is a continual process, and taking small steps every day over a long period of time makes most lasting changes. Personal transformation takes time and is not always linear. Sometimes you may take two or three steps forward, then one or two steps back. Prepare yourself for this reality and don't give up. Don't expect perfection either. Instead focus on making progress overall.

3. Transformation and conversion always involve learning new things, but you can create your own shortcut. Instead of starting from scratch, learn from the journeys and mistakes of others who have already taken the path on which you're embarking.

5. DISCUSS

In group settings, we tend to think of discussion as either debating a point or give-and-take question asking. However, there is another way to promote group discussion that digs deeper. It is best explained by seeing what happened during World War II between the State Department in the United State and homemakers.

In order to support the war effort, hamburgers, steaks, and other cuts of meat were rationed. Families were issued stamps they could use to purchase this type of meat. The State Department wanted homemakers to use as little of these cuts of meat as possible so soldiers overseas could be sent more of it. To encourage women to buy more non-rationed cuts of meat such as heart, liver, and kidneys, they enlisted Kurt Lewin, a University of Michigan researcher, to help them.

Lewin arranged to have groups of housewives hear lectures from noted authorities on the benefits of supporting the war effort, as well as cooks and dietitians on how to prepare non-rationed cuts of meat and their nutritional value. Then, he assessed their buying habits in the coming weeks. Few of the participants—only about three percent—reported using these non-rationed cuts of meat.

Lewin then tried another approach. With other groups, he had short presentations. Following these short presentations, a group leader asked how participants thought Americans could be persuaded to change their buying and eating habits. Personalizing the discussion, the group leader asked participants about their own habits, and what it would take for them to change their family's habits. Listening to each other, participants offered suggestions to one another. Over time, Lewin could see the discussion hinged on the thought of "what type of food that people like us eat." At the end of the discussion, the group leader asked them first to make a private decision about what they might consider doing differently. Following this personal reflection, the group leader asked each person if they would be willing to buy and use non-rationed cuts of meat in the coming weeks. Not everyone made a commitment. Among those who did commit, about a third of the participants followed through and made a personal change.

Lewin changed food habits by better understanding housewives' thoughts and then letting them discuss among themselves "what people like me eat." Women at the time tended to think of the non-rationed cuts of meat as "food *other people* eat." By having participants openly discuss, personally agree, and vocally commit to others, they came to a different realization about themselves that enabled them to purchase and prepare new dishes for their families.[9]

These are important considerations. In order to use the scriptures and gospel study to become better people, you need discuss how you can see yourself differently. You need to understand the implications of a scripture or gospel message for *someone like you,* and make both a personal and a public commitment as to what you will do to become more Christlike.

6. TESTIFY

An important, lasting way that you can gain spiritual knowledge and make the most of study time is by bearing testimony to each other. You will have many occasions to bear testimony and, according to President Spencer W. Kimball, many missed opportunities. When you are overly focused on giving thanks and expressing appreciation, it is a "thank-imony" not a testimony.

Truman G. Madsen, a former professor at BYU, taught that too often we *stipulate* or acknowledge three basic beliefs—the Book of Mormon is true, the gospel is restored, and prophets lead us today—rather than *testify* or give a personal witness of *how* we know such things, *when* we received this witness, and *why* it matters.

For testimonies to grow and remain robust and vibrant through time, they require constant nourishment and renewal. It is not a "once and for all" kind of thing. Our testimonies grow as we seek additional witnesses to our fundamental beliefs; to seek means to go deeper, reach further, and do more in both understanding our own testimony and expressing it to others. President Boyd K. Packer gave this important perspective on how bearing our testimony strengthens it:

A testimony is to be found in the bearing of it! Somewhere in your quest for spiritual knowledge, there is that 'leap of faith,' as the philosophers call it. It is the moment when you have gone to the edge of the light and stepped into the darkness to discover that the way is lighted ahead for just a footstep or two. . . . Can you not see that [a witness] will be supplied as you share it? As you give that which you have, there is a replacement, with increase! . . .

Bear testimony of the things that you hope are true, as an act of faith. It is something of an experiment, akin to the experiment that the prophet Alma proposed to his followers [in Alma 32]. . . .

The Spirit and testimony of Christ will come to you for the most part *when*, and remain with you only *if*, you share it. . . .

You cannot find it, nor keep it, nor enlarge it unless and until you are willing to share it. It is by giving it away freely that it becomes yours.[10]

Testimony bearing is a learning and discovery process, not merely a way to tell others about our beliefs. We get new insights ourselves, additional revelation for our own use, and answers to questions we may have as we bear testimony; the very words we need most are given when we stretch our minds and hearts and seek to express ourselves in bearing testimony. Testimony is neither a trite recitation of the same things over and over again nor an edgy declaration of fringe beliefs but instead a profound search to express how and when and why we are witnesses in the latter days for the Church of Jesus Christ of Latter-day Saints.

When President Brigham Young in 1875 called Junius F. Wells to create and lead the YMMIA (Young Men's Mutual Improvement Association), he gave similar advice about testimony bearing as both a teaching device and learning mechanism:

At your meetings you should begin at the top of the roll and call upon as many members as there is time for to bear their testimonies and at the next meeting begin where you left off and call upon others, so that all shall take part and get into the practice of standing up and saying something. Many may think they haven't any testimony to bear, but get them to stand up and they will find the Lord will give them utterance to many truths they had not thought of before. More people have obtained a testimony while standing up trying to bear it than down on their knees praying for it.[11]

Can testimony bearing become more insightful than prayer? At times, yes. Bearing testimony forces us to examine our beliefs, confront our inadequacies, and rely on the Lord to give us what we need to say in the very moment we need it. As we reach beyond our comfort zone to find the right words, they are given to us in the very hour of our need (see Doctrine and Covenants 84:85).

SUMMARY

Gospel learning is much more than memorizing facts and figures. It is also more than knowing and understanding—as important as both knowing and understanding are. It includes applying and *becoming* a new person. It is hungering and thirsting after righteousness. It is recognizing the ambiguities of the world and wrestling with them so that we can get personal insights and then testify of gospel truths. This goes well beyond the typical study and report learning process from high school. Being a good student does not make a gospel apprentice. Liz Wiseman, a business consultant and member of the Church, also emphasizes that those who cannot learn, unlearn, and relearn will be left behind as the rate of change in the world speeds up. Liz calls this "rookie smarts."[11] Being a rookie means cultivating a mindset to ask questions, seek help from others, experiment together with others on new approaches to old problems, and never being satisfied with things the way they are, but rather seeking continuous improvement.

REFERENCES

1. *Teachings of the Prophet Joseph Smith*, sel. Joseph Fielding Smith (Deseret Book, 1976), 137.

2. Neil A. Maxwell, "Jesus, the Perfect Mentor," *Ensign,* 2001.

3. "Teachings of Presidents of the Church: David O. McKay" (2003), 32.

4. See Camille Fronk Olsen's *Mary, Martha, and Me* (Salt Lake City: Deseret Book, 2006) for a fuller discussion of this topic.

5. *Teachings of the Prophet Joseph Smith,* 151.

6. Patrick Kearon, "Opening Our Hearts to Revelation," *Ensign,* August 2013, 50.

7. Joseph Campbell, *The Hero with a Thousand Faces* (Novato, CA: New World Library, 2008).

8. David A. Bednar, "Converted unto the Lord," *Ensign*, November 2012.

9. Cari Romm, "The World War II Campaign to Bring Organ Meats to the Dinner Table," *The Atlantic*, September 25, 2014.

10. Boyd K. Packer, "The Candle of the Lord," *Ensign*, January 1983, 51.

11. Junius F. Wells, "Historic Sketch of the YMMIA," *Improvement Era,* June 1925, 715.

12. Liz Wiseman, *Rookie Smarts* (New York: HarperCollins, 2014), 26.

Chapter 5

NOBODY'S PERFECT

How to take counsel without taking offense

We all like to think we are open to advice, counsel, and feedback, but accepting and applying it can be difficult. There are many different reasons why it's hard: we may question the person's motives for giving us feedback, we may become defensive and not agree with the advice, or we may even feel threatened and refuse to admit that we could do something better.

Despite these many different reasons, we also recognize, perhaps intuitively, that getting good advice from experienced leaders and teachers is fundamental to personal growth. New missionaries, in particular, realize there is much that they can learn from others, even though accepting their counsel and advice may be difficult. Elder Preston Whiting, serving in the Portugal Lisbon mission, perhaps said it best when he wrote to me:

> I've never been given so much advice in my life as when I arrived in the mission field. I don't think I was prepared to have so many people telling me what to do. It can be overwhelming. Even when I know that what someone is telling me is for my own good, sometimes it still is not easy to hear it or to put it into practice.

Since giving and getting advice on a mission is frequent and often-times good, understanding it, cultivating it, and discerning its value are all important tasks for a missionary. It's not for the fainthearted, so buckle up and fasten your seat belt, and let's dive into ways we can cultivate constructive feedback through our words and actions.

There's an old adage that states, "words can use us as much as we use them," meaning the words we choose and how we interpret others' words makes a big difference in our receptivity. For instance, the scriptures speak often about weaknesses, but in today's parlance, telling someone they have weaknesses they need to do something about may simply set their teeth on edge. This is more than a matter of semantics. Instead it's about choosing words that help convey a precise message and have a positive impact.

Ed Eyestone, former Olympic runner and current BYU Track coach, believes the word "criticism" has such a negative connotation in today's vernacular that it should be replaced by a different term: *giving direction*. As a coach, he's paid to tell athletes what to do. Sometimes they take his advice, sometimes they don't. In trying to figure out how to improve his own methods for giving advice, he had a personal experience that helped him better accept advice himself.

Ed has six daughters; some are athletic while others are not. One of them likes to perform on the stage and asked her Dad to perform with her in a community theater. He was nervous about trying something out of his comfort zone, but he auditioned for the play so they could do an activity together. To his surprise, he was given the part and was cast in the play with her. At the end of the run of the play, he had a chance to introduce his wife to George Nelson, the director. George said to Ed's wife, "Ed takes direction well." Even as a coach, he's willing to accept advice and try it out.

Everyone loves to give direction, Coach Eyestone notes. It's fun to tell others what to do and when and how to do it, he says. However, taking direction is not easy. How you respond to taking direction determines how much you can improve. If you embrace taking direction rather than view it as criticism, you likely will learn and grow. If you are devastated by direction, you are more likely to remain stuck.[1] Ultimately, taking direction well requires us to trust, experiment, and adjust. When we are open to direction, we check our pride at the door and become humbler. Only then can we truly maximize our learning potential.

So how do we learn to back off the defensive and stay open to getting direction?

TAKE A DEEP BREATH, DON'T REACT

At the first sign of getting any advice or counsel, before doing anything else—stop. Really. Try not to react at all! You'll have at least one second to stop your reaction. While one second seems insignificant in real life, it's ample time for your brain to assess a situation and simply acknowledge that you are paying attention. And in that moment, you can halt a dismissive facial expression or reactive quip, and remind yourself that you don't have to agree or disagree, or even defend or justify your situation. You just simply have to stop, take a breath, and acknowledge that you are ready to hear what is being said. It's similar to what prophets often do when the Lord speaks: affirm their readiness to hear Him.

This "readiness to hear" and connect, not simply wait for a chance to respond, is what Diarmaid MacCulloch, British historian and author of the scholarly work *Christianity: The first Three Thousand Years,* says is typical of the Lord's interactions with prophets in the Old Testament. McCullough goes further by illustrating how a "call and response" often used today in such musical formats as spirituals exemplifies this interaction. In spirituals, "call and response" simply means that one person offers an idea or throws out a phrase and others respond energetically by repeating or completing the phrase. The song "Swing Low, Sweet Chariot," the military chant "Sound Off," and the instrumental folk song "Dueling Banjos" all use a form of "call and response" to engage audiences and turn them from mere spectators to active participants. McCullough believes the scriptures use this same technique with the Lord "calling" and inviting a particular prophet—and by extension all of us—to "respond" merely by announcing our readiness to hear. [2]

Here are a few examples from the scriptures where there is a clear "call and response," a readiness to hear.

- Exodus 3:4: "And when the Lord saw that he turned aside to see, God called unto him out of the midst of the [burning] bush, and said, Moses, Moses. And he said, Here am I."
- 1 Samuel 3:4 "That the Lord called Samuel: and he answered, Here am I."
- Abraham 3:27: "And the Lord said: Whom shall I send? And one answered like unto the Son of Man: Here am I, send me. And another answered and said Here am I, send me. And the Lord said: I will send the first."

Taking a deep breath and not reacting when others offer advice is the first step in reducing their apprehension for giving you suggestions. Giving advice is hard. Make it easier for others by listening carefully and not reacting defensively. Through facial expressions and gestures, let others know you are open and want to hear more. Avoid evaluating on the spot whether you agree or not, simply encourage others giving advice to share their perspectives and feelings. You can determine later whether you want to follow their suggestions, but showing your openness by encouraging them to "say more" keeps the channels of communication open.

CHOOSE NOT TO BE OFFENDED

Once you've taken a deep breath and stepped back a bit, look for ways to communicate to the person offering advice that you are ready to genuinely listen and consider how you can improve. This does not mean you must agree with everything they will have to say. You can still reserve judgment on their advice until you can fully assimilate it.

This "engaged interest" is important; they can continue without worrying about hurting your feelings or offending you in some way. Avoid taking offense. There's an old adage that "no one can offend you without your permission." In other words, it's not what someone else says that causes offense, but how we take it that matters. We can make ourselves bulletproof simply by assuming good intentions from others and refusing to take offense.

Elder David A. Bednar said it this way in a memorable conference address:

> When we believe or say we have been offended, we usually mean we feel insulted, mistreated, snubbed, or disrespected. And certainly clumsy, embarrassing, unprincipled, and mean-spirited things do occur in our interactions with other people that would allow us to take offense. However, it ultimately is impossible for another person to offend you or to offend me. Indeed, believing that another person offended us is fundamentally false. To be offended is a *choice* we make; it is not a *condition* inflicted or imposed upon us by someone or something else.[3]

During a difficult period in the Book of Mormon when the Nephites were battling both the Lamanites and internal dissenters, Captain Moroni wrote to the Chief Judge Pahoran that he needed more troops, support, and supplies. For added emphasis, he said that he was writing "by way of condemnation" (Alma 60:2) and that if Pahoran didn't respond quickly, Moroni would stop fighting the Lamanites and instead attack the government. As it turns out, Pahoran was doing all that he could to repel a Nephite rebellion and was supporting Captain Moroni as much as he possibly could. Choosing not to be offended by the counsel he was getting from Captain Moroni, Pahoran responded by writing: "Behold, I say unto you, Moroni, that I do not joy in your great afflictions, yea, it grieves my soul. . . . And now in your epistle, you have censured me, but it mattereth not: I am not angry; but do rejoice in the greatness of your heart" (Alma 61:2, 9).

While Moroni had it all wrong, Pahoran did not get angry, refused to be offended, and reinforced their common commitment to their people and to the gospel. Pahoran looked beyond Moroni's words and saw, instead, "the greatness of [his] heart."

LISTEN FOR UNDERSTANDING

You've avoided an initial "gut reaction," and have shown engaged interest so that the person giving advice feels open with you. Well done! Now, you're ready to focus and really hear what advice they have to give so that you can figure out how to apply their suggestions and continually follow a positive direction.

As the person shares feedback with you, listen closely. Allow the person to share their complete thoughts without interruption. When they're done, repeat back what you heard. For example, "I hear you saying that you want me to try using a written lesson plan. Is that correct?"

At this point, avoid analyzing or questioning the person's assessment; instead, just focus on understanding his or her comments and perspective. Give them the benefit of the doubt here—it's difficult to give feedback to another person. Recognize that the person giving you advice may be nervous or may not express their ideas perfectly. Isaiah cautioned that we not make "a man an offender for a word, and lay a snare for him that reproveth in the gate, and turn aside the just for a thing of naught" (Isaiah 29:21; 2 Nephi 27:32). Others might not always say things just right, so look for the nuggets that make sense rather than scrutinizing their way of communication.

While there's lots of people who would like to tell us how to do things, good advice is hard to come by. Just as the Lord gives us more directions based on our receptivity, so do other people. Here's a pattern that can be used in our own personal circumstances:

For behold, thus saith the Lord God: I will give unto the children of men line upon line, precept upon precept, here a little and there a little; and blessed are those who hearken unto my precepts, and lend an ear unto my counsel, for they shall learn wisdom; for unto him that receiveth I will give more; and from them that shall say, We have enough, from them shall be taken away even that which they have (2 Nephi 28:30).

ASK FOR HELP

Advice can be a hard thing to control. It can be well-meaning or unintentional, sought out or unsolicited. Sometimes, it is helpful, while other times it can be devastating. Having a good sense of self is helpful when sorting through any advice that we may be given. All advice is not created equal so it's important to have some filters for determining the value of any particular advice. So how do we navigate between these two ends of the spectrum between helpful and detrimental advice?

First, recognize that "one size does not fit all." In other words, what may be helpful in one situation and to one person may not fit you or your circumstances. Consequently, limit the number of people from whom you get advice to those who know you well. They are in the best position to act as a sounding board, and can help sort through different points of view.

Second, offer your own perspective on any advice you may have been given to a friend or counselor and then ask for their opinion. What do you think about it? What seems on target? What are you uncertain about? What would you like to know more about? Share your thoughts on any advice you've been given, then ask for help to interpret the advice. Just as Oliver Cowdrey was told to do more than simply ask for the Lord's help, so we should do the same when sorting through any advice that we are given.

> Behold, you have not understood; you have supposed that I would give it unto you, when you took no thought save it was to ask me. (Doctrine and Covenants 9:7)

Third, experiment with suggestions that are given to you in a small way. Just as Alma encourages us to experiment with the Word of God, so we can also experiment with advice and suggestions we are given so that we "try the experiment of its goodness" (Alma 34:4).

Constructive advice is one of the best ways we learn about things that we are not doing well. When we are defensive instead of open and accepting, we miss out on opportunities to improve. Try not to tune out things you don't agree with and instead ask: what can I learn from what is being said? At the same time, don't accept all advice as if it is completely accurate. It may not be. As Paul notes, "all things edify not" (1 Corinthians

10:23). Review with a friend or companion or someone who knows you well any advice that you may be given, and test it out. When there seems to be more than one person saying the same thing, the advice is likely something that is worth paying attention to and thoughtfully considering. The scriptures give us a helpful guide in this regard:

> Without counsel purposes are disappointed: but in the multitude
> of counsellors they are established. (Proverbs 15:22)

SEEK TO EDIFY AND BE EDIFIED

The word "edify" as used in the scriptures means to "build up or strengthen." All good advice and counsel will do the same thing. It will not demean, tear down, or belittle. The world does a good enough job to pull us down and tell us that we are not good enough. It is Satan's attempt to discredit us and make us think that we can't succeed. Advice that demeans or downplays our abilities is never good advice.

> Let us therefore follow after the things which make for peace,
> and things wherewith one may edify another. (Romans 14:19)

Not long ago I was watching a junior high basketball game. The home team began trailing badly. The boys were exhausted and discouraged, but instead of encouraging each other, they began to pick on one another. Soon, they were competing more against each other than against the other team! The coach tried to help them pull together, but the boys would not listen. They were more intent on pointing out each other's faults than they were in supporting each other.

We all need each other. None of us can improve alone. But giving and accepting advice and counsel is not the same as criticizing and pointing out faults.

David's relationship with Jonathon is illustrative of a "companionship" that was mutually supportive and edifying. The scriptures tell how Jonathan loved David as his own life and how they looked out for each other. They exchanged a lifetime commitment to meet the needs of each other's families. Once, when Jonathan's father, King Saul, was searching for David to take his life, Jonathan warned David, and he was able to escape from the King. Then, Jonathan "went to David into the wood, and strengthened his hand in God" (1 Samuel 23:16). They had each other's back, but they also sought to help each other improve and become better people. They edified one another.

SUMMARY

"Hear counsel, and receive instruction, that thou mayest be wise in thy latter end" (Proverbs 19:20). We can all benefit from good advice. Still, it's not always easy to hear about things which we might need to improve upon and do better. Bill Dyer, a friend of mine who served as a Regional Representative and Dean of the business school at BYU, often said that it is always helpful to "assume good intent" from others. Doing so, makes us less defensive and more open. Further, he said, when getting feedback we should first express appreciation for it and then immediately ask for more. We don't need to accept or reject the feedback, but letting others know that it is appreciated helps us to be more open and others to be more comfortable offering advice in the future. In teaching this approach, Bill would ask students or group members to repeat after him:

Thank you very much. That's very interesting. Please tell me more.

This simple, disarming approach helps givers and receivers. Remember, counsel and instruction are given for our betterment, not for us to feel worse about ourselves for not measuring up. Recognize that others want the best for us; validate feedback you get with respected others; experiment with new behaviors or skills that may be more productive; and never give up trying to improve.

REFERENCES

1. Edward D. Eyestone, "Run Like a Horse," *YMagazine*, Winter 2016.
2. Diarmaid MacCulloch, *Christianity: The First Three Thousand Years* (New York: Penguin, 2009), 247.
3. David A. Bednar, "And Nothing Shall Offend Them," *Ensign,* October 2006. Emphasis in original.

Chapter 6

WE'RE IN THIS TOGETHER

*How to get members to join in
your missionary efforts*

Most members want to help missionaries. Sometimes we assume members don't help more because they are fearful of offending someone, or maybe they don't quite know how to share the gospel. This may be true in some cases, but with an increasing number of returned missionaries perhaps most of us are neither fearful nor uninformed. What then? What holds us back? No doubt there are as many different reasons as there are members of the Church. However, understanding members better, especially priesthood leaders and their perspective, can be a good place to start.

Perhaps Elder M. Russell Ballard identified a common sentiment when he spoke about putting our trust in the Lord when sharing the gospel:

> We know that when someone gets up to give a talk in sacrament meeting and says, "Today I'll be talking about missionary work," or perhaps even when Elder Ballard gets up in general conference and says the same thing, some of you listening may think, "Oh no, not again; we have heard this before." Now, we know that no one likes feeling guilty. Perhaps you feel you may be asked to do unrealistic things in your relationships with friends or neighbors.

With the help of the Lord, let me remove any fear you or any of our full-time missionaries may have in sharing the gospel with others.[1]

President Dallin H. Oaks has also encouraged us—both as members and missionaries—to ensure that our motives are pure and that we desire nothing but the eternal welfare of others when sharing the gospel. We can pray for this desire and know the Lord will answer our prayers if offered with sincerity and full purpose of heart.

We must be sure we act out of love, and not in any attempt to gain personal recognition or advantage. The warning against those who use a Church position to gratify their pride or vain ambition (see Doctrine and Covenants 121:37) surely also applies to our efforts to share the gospel.

President Dallin H. Oaks emphasized the importance of sharing the gospel only for the purpose of blessing the lives of others, and not for other reasons. He also asked us to stop using the term "missionary tools."[2]

How many times in a Priesthood or Relief Society or Sacrament meeting have we been part of a review of missionary tools? How often has the approach taken by the full-time missionaries seemed more about numbers and statistics and less about the humble seekers after truth whom the Lord has prepared but simply do not know where to find the gospel? Somehow, we all need to "flip the narrative" and more diligently follow the guidance given by our leaders to act out of love, with neither hypocrisy nor guile, and only for the welfare of others.

"And above all things have fervent charity among yourselves; for charity preventeth a multitude of sins." (Joseph Smith Translation, 1 Peter 4:8 [in 1 Peter 4:8, footnote *a*]).

It is a commonly accepted principle that doing things for others increases our love and commitment toward them. Often, service activities are identified for those in the community who are in need. While such societal needs are real and growing in almost every country, there are also opportunities all around us among the members of our ward and branch to follow the Savior's example and spend our time "going about doing good" (Acts 10:38). Too often missionaries overlook opportunities that are close to them to help with a lesson or teach a song in Primary or welcome a member who recently moved into the ward or branch.

Here are two examples from a case study developed by Clayton Christensen (abridged with his permission), a former Area Authority Seventy and Harvard Business School professor. Contrast the approach of the Sisters and the Elders in these two examples.

EXAMPLE 1: SACRAMENT MEETING

When the sisters arrived at 7:45, there were already about 30 people seated in the chapel. While Sister Pingree headed toward her customary seat, Sister Fulcher spotted a young couple with two small children on the other side of the chapel, and walked straight there. "Hi, I'm Sister Fulcher. Your baby is so cute! Would you mind if we sat next to you so I could oogle over her during the meeting?"

"It's good to meet you," Sister Pingree responded. Sister Pingree opened her scriptures while Sister Fulcher fired questions at Sister Palmisano. "Where do you live? Were you raised in Medford? Do your parents still live there? How about brothers and sisters? Is this one of those famous, big, close Italian families I've heard about? How did you find out about the Church? What is your present calling in the ward? Tell me about your husband. How did you meet?" It was clear that Sister Fulcher still had a long list of unasked questions when Bishop Bowen stood to open the meeting.

The Elders arrived after the meeting began and sat by themselves near the back of the chapel.

EXAMPLE 2: TEACHING THE YOUTH

In Priests Quorum, the missionaries were asked to give a lesson. They decided to teach the plan of salvation. "We want you to pretend that you are the investigator, and really give us a hard time," they said.

In the Laurel class, the full-time sister missionaries began their lesson differently.

"Rather than teach you a lesson today, we had an idea for an activity that we wanted to brainstorm with you," Sister Fulcher said. "We met an elderly widow on the bus named Frances Parnagian, and we've been teaching her the discussions. She lives alone—her son is in another part of the country. Would you girls be interested in getting a Christmas tree with us, making some decorations, and then going over to her apartment and decorating it together?"

The girls nodded their approval, and Sister Fulcher continued. "Now, there are only three of you. I think we could help your friends find more happiness in Christmas if you each invited one friend to work with you on this project. We'll be there, but we'll just try to be friends and won't try to convert them or anything. What do you think?"

RETHINKING WAYS TO SHARE THE GOSPEL

Notice what the Sisters in these two examples actually did. They didn't just talk about sharing the gospel or doing missionary work. Instead, they lived the gospel and created opportunities for others to live the gospel with them, especially in the second example. It makes a significantly different impact to engage members rather than maintain a rigid and distant relationship with them.

While living in Houston, Texas, I casually mentioned at the end of an office meeting that on Saturday I was going to can peanut butter which would be used at the Houston food bank and for members of our Church who needed temporary assistance. Several people later visited my office to ask more questions. Two colleagues even asked if they could also participate on Saturday with their families. In each case, they brought their spouse and children to the peanut butter canning event and later toured the adjacent regional Bishop's storehouse. One of these families received lessons from the missionaries and, while they were not baptized, they became advocates for the Church at work and in their local neighborhood.

Elder Dieter F. Uchtdorf encouraged members to consider natural and everyday ways we can simply share with others things we are doing which they are likely to find interesting, regardless of their interest in our beliefs. Elder Uchtdorf said this in the 2019 April general conference:

If someone asks about your weekend, don't hesitate to talk about what you experienced at church. Tell about the little children who stood in front of a congregation and sang with eagerness how they are trying to be like Jesus. Talk about the group of youth who spent time helping the elderly in rest homes to compile personal histories. Talk about the recent change in our Sunday meeting schedule and how it blesses your family. Or explain why we emphasize that this is the Church of Jesus Christ and that we are Latter-day *Saints,* just as the members of the ancient Church were also called *Saints.* In whatever ways seem natural and normal to you, share with people why Jesus Christ and His Church are important to you. Invite them to *"come and see."*[3]

Missionaries can help members see this shift in focus and emphasis. Rather than traditional methods of friendshipping often emphasized over the years of picking *certain* neighbors or friends to give a Book of Mormon or invite to a Family Home Evening, this approach focuses on talking to *everyone* about what we are *doing* (not our beliefs) and letting their interest determine what we do next. This approach of simply sharing more explicitly what we are *doing* is natural and normal, and less likely to offend anyone. Missionaries can help members see this change in emphasis, and encourage members to adopt it in their everyday conversations with others.

Rather than telling members about so-called missionary tools, missionaries can help them have more fruitful gospel conversations that allow others to ask questions about ordinary activities. Suddenly, the narrative is flipped. With a little reporting about Church-related activities, others are likely to ask more about them. Instead of members guiding the conversation, others interested in what we may be doing are now asking more questions, and we are simply responding to their expressions of interest.

This new approach changes us as members as well. We no longer need to feel guilt for not doing enough or not friendshipping more. Now, we simply need to have ordinary conversations and let others' interests drive the conversation. Even the language of sharing the gospel has changed from being called doing "missionary work" or using "missionary tools."

President Dallin H. Oaks has encouraged us to adopt this new terminology and approach, anticipating that it will avoid potential misunderstanding and focus our motivation on acting out of love rather than for any other motives. President Oaks said that he even prefers using the phrase "sharing the gospel" rather than "missionary work" because of the different connotations this phrase has in helping us simply have more explicit conversations with others about our daily activities.[2]

Some years ago, in the Texas Houston Mission where I was serving as a Counselor, we decided that there is often a negative connotation associated with the word "work." We can think of "work" as obligatory, difficult, demanding. Consider terms like:

- Home*work*
- House*work*
- Yard*work*

We decided this connotation made it more difficult to share the gospel. Since the opposite of work is fun, we started to talk about "missionary fun" instead and encouraged each other to have more "missionary fun."

Years later, when Elder Neal L. Andersen was also encouraging us to share the gospel, he told of Jackson Haight in the Boston area who told Elder Andersen about his experiences sharing the gospel online. He then told Elder Andersen "This isn't missionary work. This is missionary fun."[5]

I remember my phone lighting up with notifications from my adult children, and mission friends that now lived around the country, telling me that our use of this engaging phrase was officially validated because it was included in Elder Andersen's talk. We can all have more "missionary fun" by sharing the gospel in easy, natural ways rather than using old terms, and at times, unnecessary missionary tools.

REVERSE DINNER APPOINTMENTS

Members enjoy having missionaries for dinner, and missionaries certainly enjoy a home cooked meal. What could be nicer than to relax at a member's home, play with their children, and have a meal that is better prepared than those missionaries typically prepare for themselves? Even if the meal is simple and basic, a home-cooked meal can be a healthy and delicious alternative to missionaries cooking for themselves in their apartment. Of course, dinner appointments can also help stretch a missionary's food budget.

Many members want to show appreciation to the missionaries and consider a dinner appointment as the best expression of their heartfelt interest and care. For some members, entertaining the missionaries involves a significant financial sacrifice. For others, their schedules and circumstances make it difficult to plan a time when they can invite the missionaries over for dinner. They would like the spirit that missionaries bring in their home, but at times personal demands make it difficult for them to set up dinner appointments.

While proselyting with the missionaries in Ghana, there were many times when I was invited to a member's home and invited to stay for dinner. It pained me to see the limited sustenance available in some homes, and yet a sumptuous meal was prepared for us. In some cases, I saw children given small portions at the dinner table with stern looks from parents that seemed to say, "Don't ask for more. The missionaries are here." While I recognized the generosity that members willingly offered, I wondered if there was a better way of allowing members to express appreciation without it being so burdensome.

We prayerfully considered this dilemma at Mission Leaders Council along with ways that we might address it. When initially discussing this matter together, the zone and sister training leaders emphasized that it would be rude to refuse any offers of food or dinner appointments that might be offered. While recognizing this cultural sensitivity, I also stressed that when invited to dinner in the United States and Europe it is customary to bring a host or hostess gift as well. In my years living in West Africa, I brought a hostess gift when invited to dinner which was always appreciated. While this was new to many missionaries, they all thought it was a great idea.

As the discussion progressed, a missionary commented that if there were blessings for members who sacrificed for the missionaries by preparing dinner for us, perhaps these same blessings would be available to us as missionaries if we prepared meals for the members. While this new idea was resisted initially by some, through examples and discussion the entire Mission Leaders Council soon came to adopt the idea of regular "reverse dinner appointments." Through these reverse dinner appointments, missionaries would take meals to members rather than expect members always to prepare meals for them. During our discussion, we found two applicable scriptures on hospitality that seemed to apply as much to missionaries as to members at large:

Use hospitality one to another without grudging. (1 Peter 4:9)

Distributing to the necessity of saints; given to hospitality. (Romans 12:13)

The New Testament has many stories that embody hospitality, including the good Samaritan, the prodigal son, and the disciples on the road to Emmaus. The essence of hospitality is serving others by inviting them to eat a common meal at a common table. It is the conversation that is included during such times that can turn a simple meal into a prayer to our Heavenly Father.

Following this Mission Leaders Council, we made a concerted effort to "practice hospitality" by each missionary companionship identifying families in their ward or branch with whom they could set up "reverse dinner appointments" and take a meal to that family which the missionaries had prepared. In some cases, missionaries needed to develop cooking skills they had never mastered. In other cases, some members were initially reluctant to have the missionaries serve them. Soon both members and missionaries became enmeshed in the spirit of giving and making this service a vibrant effort. In one branch, the missionaries asked the Relief Society sisters to help them with cooking lessons. In another branch, a missionary companionship became so good at cooking banana bread that the Relief Society sisters asked these missionaries for a short cooking lesson! In these many ways, both members and missionaries in those wards and branches became more unified, missionaries built stronger relationships with members, and members supported missionaries in ways they had never done before.

Since returning from Ghana, I've shared this experience with many prospective, full-time, and ward missionaries. From Puerto Rico to

Portugal, Seattle to St. George, and Arizona to the Dominican Republic, it has been discussed at youth conferences, mission prep classes, and zone conferences with additional ideas added each time and wonderful results reported afterward. Such gospel-related hospitality is the kind of meaningful personal service that benefits the giver and the recipient.

LINGER LONGER

The Guide to the Scriptures gives this perspective on fellowship in the Church:

> For Latter-day Saints, fellowship includes offering friendly companionship, serving, uplifting, and strengthening others. ("Fellowship," Guide to the Scriptures available at churchofjesuschrist.org or the Gospel Library app)

Regardless of whether we have been members of the Church for five days or five generations, we know that we can often feel like we are "strangers and foreigners" and how good it feels to be "fellow citizens and of the household faith." We are a congregation of converts. We gladly welcome others. We know what it is like to be new, uncertain, and what a relief it can be when someone reaches their hands out to welcome us.

President Hinckley's daughter, Sister Virginia H. Pearce, while speaking at general conference, noted that the Church, like home, is a place where we are always welcome. She quoted from Robert Frost's epic poem "The Death of the Hired Man":

> Home is a place where, when you have to go there,
> They have to take you in.
> I should have called it:
> Something you somehow haven't to deserve.[6]

Missionaries can do much to promote this type of fellowship in small and simple ways—not just for investigators and new converts—but for all members of a ward or branch. Because missionaries are available to serve full-time with no other work or family commitments, they can do a lot to promote an open, genuine, and receptive culture in a ward or branch. Many times as a mission president I had local leaders call me and ask to keep certain missionaries in their unit for as long as possible. These missionaries are "difference makers" I was told time and time again.

"They not only welcome everyone, but they also pitch in and do whatever may be needed to help out in the ward," a Bishop told me.

"They lead the music or teach a lesson if a ward member is not available" another local leader said.

"They are the first to arrive at the chapel and the last to leave," a Stake President told me. "They do more than just shake hands at the doorway: they visit with members, they talk to their children, help those down the aisle who may need a little extra support."

"They don't see themselves as outsiders just passing through, as some missionaries do; but instead, see themselves as insiders; as integral to the branch,' a Relief Society president told me.

Too often in our hectic, modern times we've learned to introduce ourselves to people only in special contexts: on a doorstep, at a meeting, at the entrance to the chapel—but not in an elevator or on a bus or in the hallway. Starting a purposeful, casual conversation is a challenge for many people. It unfortunately isn't innate. Especially for introverts, getting to know people is an acquired skill.

Introverts tend to dread getting started and having meaningful small talk. They worry that they will be boring, awkward, or that they'll run out of things to say. However, after learning a few simple skills, the art of conversation can become second nature for anyone.

First off, missionaries who are uncomfortable getting acquainted with others can start by simply reducing their own anxiety. They can do this in two ways:

1. Recognize that anxiety comes from our beliefs about ourselves, not the situation. Simply saying, "I can do this" is a good place to start.

2. Then ask, "What's the worst thing that can happen? If they don't like me, so what?" Addressing our own negative self-talk can get us on a positive track.

Second, good conversationalists channel their own curiosity, and show genuine interest in others. When asking "How are you?" or "How was your weekend?" listen carefully to what the individual has to say, maintain eye contact, and follow up on something the other person said. There is no right or wrong way to start such conversations. Simply find something specific the person said and follow up on it.

Third, ask questions. The best way to start conversations *and* keep them going is simply by asking questions. We all enjoy talking about ourselves, and asking questions; let others do just that. Here's a few examples that can be helpful in any Church greeting:

- Do you live nearby?
- What do you like best about living here?
- Who are your closest neighbors who are members?
- What's something interesting about the area?
- What community events or activities do you like in the area?
- Do you have relatives who live nearby? Tell me about them.

None of these questions are intrusive, all of them are possible ways to let someone else get started talking and for you to show interest by asking additional follow up questions.

Sometimes missionaries are active in greeting new people at church, but less active talking to them after the service is over. Post-church time is an excellent opportunity to discuss a lesson, see if there are questions they can answer, or even assist large families with getting their children from their classes. Before church begins, many families and others are rushing to their seats. After church, there is less pressure to get somewhere, and it is a greater opportunity simply to get acquainted, visit, and fellowship.

While "linger longer" potluck events are often used in young single adult wards or branches as a way of getting acquainted, the concept can apply broadly to missionaries without requiring any kind of food or formal activity. Like many things in the gospel, it's the little things that matter. President Spencer W. Kimball occasionally quoted the German poet Goethe who said: "When I come to think of the importance of little things, I am convinced there are no little things." Linger longer doesn't have to be a major production. Instead it's looking for ways to visit with members about a class or quorum discussion, share insights with youth about a gospel topic, or follow the Savior's example of "going about doing good" (Acts 10:38) among those who have already made sacred covenants.

We all want to feel welcome at church. No one wants to go to a place where they feel unwanted. Gospel instruction at Sacrament meetings as well as in quorums and classes is essential. But so is a sense of belonging and feeling like we are part of something bigger than ourselves. President Gordon B. Hinckley once said that every new member "needs three things: a friend, a responsibility, and nurturing with 'the good word of God.'"[7] Long-time members need these same three things. Missionaries can be a catalyst for engaging any ward or branch by fellowshipping more, promoting a sense of community simply by lingering longer, starting conversations with everyone, and serving members of the church in small and simple ways.

As the Apostle Paul noted:

> For by one Spirit are we all baptized into one body, whether we be Jews or Gentiles, whether we be bond or free. . . . For the body is not one member, but many. (1 Corinthians 12:13–14)

SUMMARY

Full-time and member missionaries are partners in bringing the gospel to others. As President Thomas S. Monson emphasized:

> "Now is the time for members and missionaries to come together, to work together, to labor in the Lord's vineyard to bring souls unto Him. He has prepared the means for us to share the gospel in a multitude of ways, and He will assist us in our labors if we will act in faith to fulfill His work."[8]

REFERENCES

1. M. Russell Ballard, "Put Your Trust in the Lord" *Ensign,* November 2013, 32.

2. Dallin H. Oaks, "Sharing the Gospel," *Ensign,* November 2001, 8.

3. Dieter F. Uchtdorf, *"Missionary Work: Sharing What Is In Your Heart,"* *Ensign*, May 2019.

4. Oaks, "Sharing the Gospel," 8.

5. Neil L. Andersen, "It's a Miracle," *Ensign*, May 2013, 79.

6. Virginia H. Pearce, "Ward and Branch Families: Part of Heavenly Father's Plan for Us," *Ensign*, November 1993; quoting Robert Frost, "The Death of the Hired Man" lines 118–20, available at poetryfoundation.org.

7. Gordon B. Hinckley, "Converts and Young Men," *Ensign,* May 1997.

8. Thomas S. Monson, *The Work of Salvation: Worldwide Leadership Broadcast,* June 2013; quoted in "Hastening the Work of Salvation," *Ensign*, October 2013, 38.

Chapter 7

IMAGINE THAT

*Shifting gears toward more visual
teaching and engaged learning*

Elder David A. Bednar has written and spoken extensively on the kind
of teaching and learning that leads to conversion and the mighty
change of heart that missionaries seek to facilitate for investigators. He
emphasizes that teaching is not telling, talking, or lecturing. It requires
much more than the transmission of information, knowledge, and experiences. In his book *Act in Doctrine,* he notes:

> Teaching the gospel in the Lord's way requires observing, listen-
> ing, and discerning as prerequisites to talking. . . . As we observe,
> listen, and discern we can be given "in the very hour that portion
> that shall be meted unto every man" (Doctrine and Covenants
> 84:85).[1]

While not extremely complicated, these are not simple skills to
master and require time, practice, and periodic reassessment just like the
development of any other skill. If all we do is talk and tell, we will neither
engage investigators nor teach gospel principles. Rather, Elder Bednar
notes, we will simply be sitting in front of investigators or standing in
front of a group and talking to ourselves.

We learn in different ways. Some of us are aural learners—we prefer
listening to a story or topic in order to grasp its details. Others are

primarily abstract or introspective learners and need time by themselves to process a new idea or concept. However, most of us are primarily, or at least secondarily, visual learners: we conceptualize what we can see. We often recite that "a picture is worth a thousand words" as an example of the benefits of seeing in order to understand.

Angela, who recently served in the Spain Las Palmas Mission, noted how sometimes the people and teaching methods we think may work best may actually require us to reassess how to approach each new teaching opportunity.

> A mission is a great time to learn that your preconceived notions about things are often wrong. This is true of your role as a missionary, the people you teach, the areas you should work in, and teaching methods. You need to develop an open mind to be able to see the potential in others, even when the current reality looks difficult or unpromising. Listen to the people you teach. You aren't really there to 'teach by pouring information into their head, but you are there to listen to them, to listen to the Spirit, and to help them better their lives.

Cami, a returned missionary from the Dominican Republic Santiago Mission added that beyond teaching the gospel, the purpose of missionaries is to find ways to fully bless the lives of people they meet. This perspective changes and ultimately increases their effectiveness.

> There's a reason someone talks to the missionaries. Listen to find out what their reasons are, and see how those reasons line up with the message you are bringing. Would the church be a positive influence in their lives? If so, they will probably progress. But if they don't progress, you should still listen and serve them. Don't internalize rejection. It's not you they are rejecting. Maybe they just aren't prepared to hear the gospel. Maybe it's not a good fit for them today. If you want what's best for them, you will see them as a whole person, not just a means to achieving your own results.

OBJECT LESSONS

The Savior often used parables to teach—imagery that his listeners could relate to—such as a woman losing a coin, a shepherd looking for a lost sheep, or a sower casting seed into soil. The Savior used actual objects to make a point or teach a lesson, such as asking hearers to bring Him a coin and then describe whose image was on it, asking a woman at a well to draw water for him and then referring to himself as a well of Living Water, or feeding the five thousand and then teaching about the Bread of Life. He used ordinary objects around Him to teach divine truths.

When we use tangible objects around us to teach abstract principles we are engaging investigators in visual teaching methods. In addition to using physical objects to teach, visual lessons can also employ videos, pictures, drawings, diagrams, reenactments, whiteboards, games, handouts, role plays, case studies, and many other visually and physically engaging teaching techniques.

Is it possible to imagine a more visually oriented and optically stimulated period of time in history than our own times? Having grown up with television, video games, computer graphics, and smartphones, are we not all becoming visual learners in an increasingly visually stimulated world?

Rather than decry these changes in society and the world, perhaps as missionaries we can incorporate visual teaching and engaged learning as much as possible in our own approach to gospel instruction to promote testimony building and conversion. Just as the Savior used physical objects that were at hand and incorporated them into his teaching methods, we can do the same. When He was on a boat in the Sea of Galilee, He said the Kingdom of God was like a fishing net. Later, He told His listeners to consider the lilies, the sparrows, and the hairs on their head. Jesus referred to a fig tree, a mustard tree, yeast, salt, a vineyard, money, and other things from everyday life to reveal spiritual truths. When He spoke of a watchman on a tower, He may have been near a vineyard. When He said, "consider the sparrow," there were likely sparrows nearby. When He taught the parable of the sower, there may have been a sower in the next field where Jesus was teaching.

Missionaries have historically taught using visual teaching methods that were available to them. For more than forty years, flannel boards were the standard used by full-time missionaries. They were eventually replaced by flip charts as the common teaching mode before *Preach My Gospel* was adopted. Now, missionaries in various parts of the world have access to iPads, tablets, or smartphones to assist in teaching contacts and investigators. In Preach My Gospel itself, missionaries learn through visual examples and illustrations that proliferate throughout the manual. In addition, visual depictions from "The District" videos provide hands-on examples of teaching methods, and personal and companionship study. Methods used to instruct missionaries are great examples of the shift to visual teaching and engaged learning from prior missionary development handbooks. In addition, videos, pamphlets, and Gospel Art are available to help us use visual teaching methods in conveying gospel principles.

GETTING STARTED

In the *Teaching in the Savior's Way* manual, there is a section on using art, music, and visuals to teach the gospel effectively. This instructional guide for teachers emphasizes that the art and objects we use in teaching gospel principles should be more than mere decorations; they should help learners understand gospel doctrines. The *Gospel Art Book* contains many images that can help investigators visualize concepts or events. In addition, various gospel paintings can recreate past events for us or enable us to visualize future events that may soon occur. *The Second Coming* painting by Harry Anderson, for example, can help learners ponder how they will feel when the Savior returns. Dramatizing the parable of the prodigal son or other scriptural events is another visual way to help learners understand what it means to forgive someone who has strayed. Paintings, cases studies, movies, and other visual depictions are now readily available through the internet or specialized apps such as Gospel Media, the Tree of Life AR, Church News, Scripture Stories, or other apps that can be easily downloaded.

Brother Randall L. Ridd said, "The divine purpose of technology is to hasten the work of salvation, . . . to use these great tools to take [the Lord's] work to the next level, to share the gospel."

Technology can be a blessing or an obstacle to gospel learning depending on how it is used. As Elder Ridd notes, it can be the means to take the work of salvation to the next level, to fundamentally transform our teaching, and to enrich the lives of both missionaries and investigators.[2] There are many tools available to assist us in this teaching transformation. The Church has created a Gospel Media library on its website with dozens of media related tools to enhance visual teaching and learning. A lot of the resources available in the Gospel Media library can also be found in the Gospel Library and Gospel Media apps. Here are three examples of resources on the Gospel Media library along with ways that missionaries can use them in conveying their message and answering questions:

- Answer common questions by watching the Basic Beliefs videos.
- Share your testimony with investigators and then view videos of testimonies shared by members from around the world.
- Show a feature film video to build gospel understanding or address expressed concerns.

PLANNING AHEAD

Visual teaching and engaged learning are more than using technology or relatable objects to convey information and stimulate personal conversion. Like any tool, technology is the most effective when used at the right time and in the right way. Abraham Maslow once said that having many tools enables a teacher to be the most effective. If teachers only have a hammer, he once said, they tend to treat everything as if it were a nail. Having a variety of tools and using the right tool at the right time increases our effectiveness in conveying gospel messages.

Elder Dallin H. Oaks spoke of the importance of preparing and planning ahead in the October 1999 general conference. He said, "a gospel teacher will prepare diligently and strive to use the most effective means of presenting the prescribed lessons,"[3] rather than simply deliver a message with rote words and tried presentation methods.

We know the importance of teaching with the Spirit to guide us not only in what we teach, but also in selecting the tools we utilize to teach. The scriptures remind us that we should "teach the principles of my gospel . . . as they shall be directed by the Spirit . . . And if ye receive not the Spirit ye shall not teach" (Doctrine and Covenants 42:12–14). A missionary may teach profound truths but unless the Spirit is present, these things will not be powerfully impressed upon the investigator's soul. When the Spirit is present in a missionary discussion, "the power of the Holy Ghost carrieth [the message] unto the hearts of the children of men" (2 Nephi 33:1).

In planning in advance for any missionary discussion, here's three steps that can help you create a visually stimulating message by asking yourself:

- What PHYSICAL items are in the lesson? Would the lesson be enhanced if I showed some of them? How could I get, find, or construct those objects or things?
- What GOSPEL CONCEPTS are in the lesson that could be represented by objects, drawings, or pictures?
- What EXPERIENCE or activity could I use to promote personal reflection and commitment building?

Asking these questions helps you notice available objects, materials or details that can be used to help convey your message. Here's a simple example.

While proselytizing with a pair of missionaries in a small village in Ghana, we were hurrying to an appointment and decided to take a short cut along a sandy, dirt path. We greeted other people along the way and wished them a good day. There were few white men in this area and rarely had villagers seen a grey-haired man in a white shirt and tie walking with two young Africans, so we had many astonished looks as we walked along the footpath. About halfway to our planned appointment, a middle-aged man stopped us. He wanted to know who we were and why I was walking rather than riding in a car. After telling him that we were missionaries, he cautiously started a gospel conversation with us. Hesitantly at first, he said that he had been attending the Methodist church for more than fifteen years and he could not grasp how God could be three personages and yet one Spirit. It seemed like a mass of confusion to him. He had asked visiting pastors as well as the local pastor in the village and none of their answers satisfied him.

At this point, I asked if he was acquainted with the account of Jesus's baptism in the Bible. He said he was familiar with it and began to quote it from memory. As he did, I got down on the ground and recreated the scene from the Bible as he spoke. Drawing stick figures, I showed the river Jordan, Jesus and John, the voice of God from the heavens, and the Holy Ghost descending like a dove from the sky. He stared at my crude drawing. Over and over, he remarked to himself about these scripture verses which he could quote from memory, but it was as if he were comprehending them for the first time. He asked us not to disturb the drawing. He walked around it while talking to himself. Then, we asked if the missionaries could make an appointment to visit him and tell him about other gospel principles. He asked if they would make a drawing for him on a piece of paper like the one I had made in the sand. Laughingly, one of the elders said, "We'll make other drawings for you to keep that will answer many questions about our Heavenly Father's plan for us." The missionaries were able to teach him over the course of the next three months using a variety of visual learning tools, and he was then baptized into the Church.

MAKING CONNECTIONS

There is an old adage that suggests "people don't care how much you know until they know how much you care." Missionaries are much more than simple dispensers of gospel lessons. For many individuals looking into the Church, missionary discussions are the best part of their day. It is a chance to think deeply with others, share personal feelings openly, and explore profound spiritual promptings without being judged. As missionaries, it is vital to recognize that investigators lead a life outside of the discussions that we have with them. Missionaries need to help bridge any gaps between these new gospel experiences and the investigators' everyday lives. Showing interest in this "other life" is a beginning, but showing interest alone is not enough. Somehow, we must connect deeply and independently through the Holy Ghost with each person we teach.

In the Book of Acts, an angel directs Philip to leave Jerusalem and "go toward the south." That's it. Just go south. That's all he was told. When he did as instructed, he met an Ethiopian who was in his chariot reading Isaiah.

> And Philip ran thither to him, and heard him read the prophet Esaias, and said, Understandest thou what thou readest? And he said, How can I, except some man should guide me? (Acts 8:30–31)

Philip then climbed into the chariot beside the Ethiopian and they began visiting. Philip was directed by the Spirit but met the Ethiopian only after noticing what he was reading. He then asked him a question based on what he saw the Ethiopian doing. Philip wasn't directed by the angel to meet an Ethiopian. He had to figure that part out on his own. But he noticed what was happening around him, and asked this stranger a simple question based on observing his actions. Philip was curious. He asked questions. He was conversational, and he displayed genuine interest.

Getting acquainted with those we teach is not just a prelude to teaching them. It is fundamental to the teaching process. Making connections with strangers is not all that difficult if we put in sincere effort. Noticing others' interests, their hobbies, their family, and asking questions is a really good start to getting connected. Then, tell them about something you are interested in and like to do. Share your passion for a hobby or activity so they get acquainted with you as well. The more we share something about ourselves, the more likely others will share with us.

Too many missionaries focus only on the lesson or topic for discussions as if it's just another task that needs to get done. But it's really not. It's about seeing a person of great worth, inestimable worth —regardless of their circumstances—and taking the time to really get to know them. Let your own best self come out, and find out what you may have in common with them. Don't try to force it, but find out what's on their minds, what they like to talk about with their friends, and what they want to know about you.

TEACHING LIKE THE SPIRIT

The scriptures and modern-day prophets remind us to teach with the Spirit using the most effective means available to convey gospel messages. The Book of Mormon also gives us a dramatic example in 1 Nephi 11 of how the Spirit teaches in which it illustrates some important teaching methods.

The chapter begins with Nephi pondering and wanting to know more about a vision which his father Lehi had seen and shared with his family. As he was pondering, Nephi was carried away by the Spirit unto a high mountain.

2 And the Spirit said unto me: Behold, what desirest thou?

After a series of questions, the Spirit told him to look upon a scene that the Spirit would then use to teach Nephi.

8 And it came to pass that the Spirit said unto me: Look! And I looked and beheld a tree.

Following a discussion on the tree and its importance, the Spirit again directed Nephi's attention to a visual image:

12 And it came to pass that he said unto me: Look! And I looked as if to look upon him, and I saw him not; for he had gone from before my presence.

13 And it came to pass that I looked and beheld the great city of Jerusalem, and also other cities.

In this chapter from the Book of Mormon, the Spirit, through a series of visual representations and inspired questions, reinforces, clarifies, and explains what various scenes mean and how they apply to Nephi and his family. Thirteen different times the Spirit of the Lord directs Nephi "to look" while teaching him. In the process of looking, Nephi saw the mother of the Savior, the rod of iron, the tree of life, and the Lamb of God—all visual representations that enhanced both his understanding and his recall.

Most missionaries encourage discussion when presenting a visual aid, but we need to go a step further. For example, we can ask investigators to share how the visual representation reinforces—or challenges—what they previously knew or accepted as true, much like my earlier example about the misconceptions of the Godhead. Drawing in the sand helped the man on the footpath in Ghana to reconsider past teachings about the nature of the Godhead. Using visual learning methods is an ideal time to highlight any blind spots or confusion related to gospel doctrines that investigators may have.

Frankly, accepting the gospel and allowing the Spirit to convert someone requires a certain amount of "unlearning"—giving up something that we thought we knew. This can be difficult. The man on the footpath had been taught the concept of the Trinity—the supposed oneness of Heavenly Father, Jesus Christ, and the Holy Ghost—was correct. He had to unlearn what he had been taught and then learn something new. A simple drawing helped him see that what he had been taught could not be correct. A new understanding through the representation of Jesus's baptism drawn in the sand gave him an entirely new perspective.

How do we go about unlearning the things we think we know? This isn't a trivial task. New information helps. But showing how old ways of thinking don't make sense requires time, patience, and often some kind of visual clarity. "It ain't what you know that gets you into trouble," the humorist Mark Twain once said. "It's what you know for sure that just ain't so."

A useful way of helping someone unlearn is through verbal, visual, and activity immersion. This approach works much like learning a foreign language. A person can practice conjugating verbs and reading, writing, and speaking in a language lab, but they'll only retain so much. On the other hand, if we fully immerse ourselves in the new language and flood our thoughts and actions with it rather than worrying about translating from the new language to English (or our native language), we will learn quicker and squeeze out old thoughts with new ones. Similarly, frequent visits by missionaries to contacts and investigators not only allows them to ask questions and get answers consistently, but also allows them to examine old assumptions and old ways of thinking and replace them with new information. This new way of thinking is part of the repentance process.

The Bible Dictionary defines repentance this way: "The Greek word of which the translation denotes a change of mind, a fresh view about

God, about oneself, and about the world." It is a fresh view and change of mind from old ways of thinking and looking at the world, to new ways of looking at it that require both unlearning and relearning. This process is facilitated by visual images, thought-provoking activities, and immersive experiences that lead to greater receptivity to the promptings of the Holy Ghost.

COME AND SEE

When Nathanael questioned whether any good thing could come from Nazareth, Phillip simply replied: "Come and see" (John 1:46). Rather than try to persuade or discuss, sometimes the best approach in sharing the gospel is simply an invitation to "come and see." An important way to invite others to "come and see" is by promoting open houses at church buildings, and conducting street displays at appropriate locations.

During the 2013 Mission Presidents Seminar, each member of the First Presidency urged new mission presidents and their wives to regularly sponsor open houses at Church facilities similar to visitors' centers at major temple sites. In addition to the First Presidency, Elder David F. Evans, then managing director of the missionary department at the time, stressed that we need to adapt to the new realities of people mostly away from their homes during the day, and often living behind a "big gate" which makes traditional proselyting unavailable. He urged mission presidents to sponsor tours at Church buildings, provide displays near chapels, and conduct open houses with members as often as possible in response to these new realities.

The format and invitations for open houses must also reflect the changing times. Contemporary invitations and programs that are upbeat and colorful will be compelling for casual contacts and ordinary acquaintances alike. Open houses might include the following:

- *Displays:* Stylish photos of members, their families, temples, activities, and ordinances that allow new converts and other Church members to offer both explanations and testimonies

- *Discussions*: Separate discussions by missionaries on key gospel principles that allow for simultaneous events to proceed on different schedules without interfering with each other.
- *Music*: Singing hymns and performing instrumental music can prompt visitor's hearts to receive the Spirit at a deeper level than sometimes is possible through the use of words.
- *Food:* Food is an incentive that never ceases to fail. "Food is love," my wife likes to say. Even the apostle Peter encouraged the Saints to "Use hospitality one to another without grudging" (1 Peter 4:9) whenever possible.

The meeting after the meeting: Debriefing what works and why is an essential step in improving our efforts. It is often overlooked or neglected altogether. Identifying three to five things that made a difference and three to five things where improvement could be made will both reduce defensiveness and increase effectiveness.

Enabling the involvement of new as well as longer-term members can be powerful. During each open house, missionaries would proselyte on the street, inviting passersby to "Come and See" the open house and escort them to the building where colorful displays were set up. New members would serve best by standing beside these displays and explaining to visitors what they mean, along with offering their own testimony. While conducting an open house in Dansoman, near Accra in Ghana, a woman with her six-year-old son told this to me as she left the open house:

Initially, I was reluctant to go into your building. But once inside, I saw ordinary people there—just like me. They were in charge, it seemed, and talking about their beliefs. In my church, that would never happen. Only people with money or degrees speak at my church, not ordinary people. If you are a woman, especially, no one listens to you at my church. But I saw women—just like me—and ordinary men—not rich, not well educated—who were talking about the scriptures. I felt like a veil of shame had been taken from my head. I want to learn more. I want this for me and my son.

As promised by the First Presidency, the open houses we sponsored were enormously successful. After one open house, more than sixteen people came to church the next day. Fourteen of them were later baptized. They came, they saw, they joined. Through these experiences, members and investigators alike gained or strengthened their testimonies by sharing the good news of the gospel together.

MUSIC

We believe in music and the power it has to move us and teach us. We don't have to be accomplished singers or performers to sing the hymns of Zion. Singing these hymns can be used as a powerful way to teach the gospel to investigators as well as fellow missionaries. In the First Presidency Preface to our hymnbook, it says:

> Some of the greatest sermons are preached by the singing of hymns. Hymns move us to repentance and good works, build testimony and faith, comfort the weary, console the mourning, and inspire us to endure to the end.[4]

Good music has the wonderful power to excite, console, cheer, tug at our heartstrings and even take our breath away. Its universal appeal has no national boundaries—unlike verbal languages—since it can speak directly to our hearts and emotions through the power of the Spirit. It can enrich our souls and supplement any gospel or missionary lesson. As Alma notes,

> And now behold, I say unto you, my brethren, if ye have experienced a change of heart, and if ye have felt to sing the song of redeeming love, I would ask, can ye feel so now? (Alma 5:26)

When turning away from the ordinary things of the world and turning toward our Heavenly Father, we are able to "sing the song of redeeming love." Redemption happens as we turn our lives over to the Lord.

The children of Israel saw the mighty power that the Lord had unleashed against the Egyptians, and they were filled with awe before Him. They put their faith in the Lord and in His servant, Moses. Like a shepherd, Moses led the children of Israel away from Egypt and to the mountain of the Lord where God himself dwelt. They were redeemed physically and spiritually from the bondage of the Egyptians.

Music can similarly release us from the bondage of everyday cares and worries and lift us to a higher, more celestial level—both missionaries and investigators alike. At one point in the Ghana Accra West Mission, we had missionaries from as many as twenty-six different countries. Companion differences were inevitable. Language, customs, food, and habits are not the same across international borders, and simply putting two inexperienced young adults together and expecting them to mesh was not easy and sometimes not even possible. At times, talking things out simply doesn't work either. As much as we might hope that direct and open communications solves all problems, this is not always the case. At times, more indirect approaches can be even more effective than a "full frontal assault." I often encouraged indirect approaches—such as identifying triggers that provoked differences, reframing differences in new ways, or simply overlooking irritators—when companions were having difficulties together, and I always suggested that they have a prayer and sing a hymn before any companionship inventory. Elder Kiwanuka took singing an initial hymn to an extreme with a remarkable result when he had a companion who was homesick and having difficulty adjusting to missionary life. Here's what he wrote to me in his weekly letter:

> My new companion was so discouraged and frustrated. We came back to the apartment in the afternoon to recover because he was not feeling the spirit at all and would burst into tears simply when walking down the street. I sat on his bed and tried to encourage him. I told him how much I admired him and his gospel knowledge, his perseverance, his willingness to work hard. Nothing I said had any impact. I felt prompted to pull out my hymn book. I asked if he would sing with me. He refused. No matter. I sang by myself. First one hymn, then another, and another. Finally, he joined in with me. We sang hymns that we liked and talked about what each of them meant to us and memories they aroused. We sang and talked for a long time. It turned everything around. He felt the Spirit and we went out proselytizing and had a great day together.

Elder Kiwanuka was using the power of music to reduce stress and reorient his companion who was anxious and unsure of his ability to live and serve in a foreign country. In fact, there is a growing body of evidence that music can be helpful in many different types of situations. It can even improve medical outcomes. The Harvard Medical School issued a report showing that in controlled clinical trials of people having colonoscopies, cardiac angiography, or knee surgery, those who listened to music before their procedure had less anxiety and less need for sedatives. People who listened to music in the operating room reported less discomfort during their procedure. And those who heard music in the recovery room used less opioid medication for pain. Music has many benefits and can be used in many creative ways.[5]

SUMMARY

Teachable moments abound. They go well beyond the typical lesson that missionaries give to investigators. While these lessons will always be the fundamental building blocks for teaching the gospel, there are many other occasions and methods that missionaries can share their testimonies and do the work of the Lord: for themselves, their companions, members, and investigators. Through our words, actions, planned and unplanned activities, we are always teaching. Elder Dieter. F. Uchtdorf often has noted a saying attributed to St. Francis of Assisi: "Preach the gospel at all times and if necessary, use words."[6]

Elder Uchtdorf reminds us through this saying that there are many different ways to teach the gospel. St. Francis of Assisi practiced this same teaching dexterity by often going outside church buildings to plazas and pastures. He broke standard conventions by teaching in ways that caught the people's attention through art, music, interaction, visual aids, and displays just as missionaries can do today. He taught people, not lessons.

REFERENCES

1.   David A. Bednar, *Act in Doctrine: Spiritual Patterns for Turning from Self to Savior* (Deseret Book, 2012).

2. Randal L. Ridd "The Choice Generation," *Ensign,* May 2014, 58.

3. Dallin H. Oaks, "Gospel Teaching," *Ensign,* November 1999.

4. "First Presidency Preface to our Hymns," *Hymns,* ix.

5. Beverly Merz, "Healing through Music," *Harvard Health Blog,* November 5, 2015. Health.Harvard.edu/blog/healing-through-music-201511058556.

6. St. Francis of Assisi, in William Fay and Linda Evans Shepherd, *Share Jesus without Fear* (1999), 22; referred to in Dieter F. Uchtdorf, "A Word for the Hesitant Missionary," *Ensign*, February 2013, 4.

Chapter 8

YOU CAN GET ALONG
WITH ANYONE

How to create a "companionable" relationship

When you are with the same person 24/7 it can be exhilarating, exhausting, and sometimes extremely difficult. Certainly, sometimes it might be easier just to do things on your own and not be bothered with a companion, but life is filled with all kinds of relationships. Friends, parents, siblings, neighbors, co-workers, you name it—and the better able we are to figure out how to get along with others, the happier we will be. The good news? Learning to get along with others is an acquired and applicable skill. Some people may "get it" more easily, but for everyone there are skills we can learn that will help us make bad relationships agreeable, good relationships better, and all relationships consistent with the Savior's admonition to love our neighbor—and yes, even a difficult companion.

Sometimes mission presidents put two missionaries together so that a stronger companion will strengthen a weaker one. In Doctrine and Covenants 84:106, we read:

> And if any man among you be strong in the Spirit, let him take with him that is weak, that he may be edified in all meekness, that he may become strong also.

On the surface, this doesn't always make for an ideal relationship. Stronger missionaries may feel like they are constantly dragging their companions around, trying to get them to do the things they should do. Weaker missionaries may feel like they are always getting told what to do. Could there be a better formula for tension and disagreement? For not getting along?

The key to getting along with almost anyone is to avoid actions that diminish others, and replace getting annoyed with getting connected. Of course, sincerity is key. Most people can see through flattery and insincerity. Mindset matters. It starts with believing that even a companion with whom you don't get along is of *infinite worth*. Changing your mindset helps other things fall into place. But actions also matter and sometimes doing things differently changes how you think about a person or a situation. Sometimes, you may have to "fake it until you make it." You can do this by serving your companion since we grow to love those we serve. Genuine service breaks down barriers.

To get started, let's look at three things to *avoid* or *stop* doing, then at a few things we can *start* doing, maybe in some different ways than in the past. These three primary "irritators" can shift a relationship from neutral to reverse—or even, if not properly addressed, keep it going backward if it's already headed in the wrong direction. After looking at these three irritators, we'll then focus on three proactive ways to promote a great relationship with your companion.

GETTING ANNOYED, AND WHAT TO DO ABOUT IT

Some people just get under our skin. In some cases, we may not even know why they bother us. It could be something they do or maybe even something or someone they remind us of with whom we didn't get along with in the past. No matter the reason, start with the fact that there's something going on that's driving a wedge between you and them. When it's your companion that's the source of your aggravation, acknowledging there is a problem is the first step in doing something about it. This doesn't mean you start by saying something to them. In fact, at this point it's simply your problem; you are the one who is irritated, annoyed, or aggravated—not your companion. So, start with yourself. Own the problem. This doesn't make you a bad person. Quite the opposite. It makes you a good person for acknowledging that things could be better, and you are the one who needs to do something about it. Then, ask yourself "how might the things I'm doing contribute to the tension between us? Am I rolling my eyes when the other says something I don't like? Am I sighing audibly? Or grimacing?" You may hardly be aware of the little things you do that are off-putting and adding fuel to the fire between you and your companion.

Fundamentally, we choose to be annoyed or not be annoyed by things others do. It's always a choice that we make. Knowing this fact doesn't necessarily mean that we'll always be able to control our feelings or our decisions. But it's a start. It gives us perspective.

There's an old phrase about not letting things get your goat. Or, maybe said in a more colorful way, "someone can't get your goat unless they know where it is tied." The origin of this last phrase may be helpful in considering how you might handle little irritations from others. It seems in the past that racehorse owners would tie a goat in a stall near a revved up racehorse just before a big race to calm the horse down. Occasionally, competitors would sneak into the barn and untie the goat, thereby agitating the racehorse. To avoid getting caught, they needed to slip into the horse's stall, find where the goat was tied, and quickly untie it before the goat began bleating. If someone has "got your goat," they know how to undo what makes you calm, it's not just about someone who irritates you.

This distinction is important. You can reprogram your brain to stay calm regardless of any circumstances. Once you recognize that you are in charge of your emotions—whether you get irritated, annoyed, or aggravated at your companion or others—you can keep your goat tied, stay calm, and deliberately choose an alternative response. You can *choose happy.*

R-E-S-P-E-C-T
FIND OUT WHAT IT MEANS TO ME

Years ago, Aretha Franklin garnered a Grammy award for her song "Respect." The chorus begins as she spells out the word "respect" and then sings: "Find out what it means to me." This is great advice! Being disrespectful with our words or actions is one of the ways missionary companions can unknowingly sabotage the companionship.

We may be acting or speaking disrespectfully in ways in which we are almost unaware of what we are doing. Often, someone will be hurt when another person never intended any harm or disrespect. These unintentional "hurts" are the worst because they fester and degrade a relationship, and neither companion may be aware of what is happening. They may only know that there is something going on and it's causing a strained relationship. What are the ways we unintentionally show disrespect? Here's a short list of common ways we may unintentionally snub a companion, a member, an investigator, or others:

- **Not paying attention to someone who is speaking to you**
- **Using a condescending or patronizing tone of voice**
- **Raising your voice when responding**
- **Being unresponsive or ignoring others' comments**
- **Changing the subject or disregarding others preferences**
- **Making others an "offender for a word" by focusing on their words instead of their intent**

There's something incredibly ironic about interpersonal relationships, occurring time and time again between missionary companions: the closer we feel toward someone, the less likely we are to listen respectfully to them. It's sometimes called the "closeness-communication bias," and over time it can be incredibly disruptive between missionary companions. Once we know someone well enough to feel close to them we have a tendency to believe that we already know in advance what they are likely to say. It's similar to when we travel a familiar road: we already know the route, so we don't notice familiar signs or scenery. But people are always changing, and none of us are completely the same as we were last month, last week, or even yesterday. This closeness-communication bias is especially pronounced among missionary companions because they spend virtually every waking minute together, and they have the same experiences together.

Staying connected to someone—especially when we are with them all of the time—requires taking time to think twice (and not assume) by asking often, "Hey, wait a minute, is this really what you mean to say?" We don't do that enough—especially between missionary companions because we assume we already know what they meant.

So, what can we do to avoid this closeness-communication bias between missionary companions? The best way is through "everyday talk" and then actually listening to the responses of your companion. Too often companions reduce their conversations to logistics: "when is our next appointment?" and "who is going to teach which part of the lesson?" What often gets left out is what's really on your companion's mind. This should be the content of a companionship inventory instead of either small talk or a list of interpersonal grievances. More often than not, companionship inventories produce negative results and strained relationships either because they are too superficial or too intense.

COMPANIONSHIP INVENTORIES

Companionship inventories, or check-ins on how things are going, hold great promise. When companions open up to each other about their own struggles, fears, hopes, and joys in their everyday missionary activities these inventories can be effective. Companionship inventories can focus on mission rules—in which case both missionaries can join equally in comparing what they are doing to what is required as they set goals to improve. Additionally, these inventories can focus on ways to get better at finding, teaching, and fellowshipping. A more subjective assessment can be the basis for improving as missionaries, but it can also be the source of conflict and hurt feelings.

These subjective discussions should **not** focus on what's *wrong* with the other person nor should they become merely another daily or weekly planning session requirement. Instead, during a companionship inventory, each companion should focus on his or her mission-related **desires**, **interests**, and **goals** and then ask for *input, advice,* and *suggestions* from the other companion. This forward-looking focus begins with each companion starting out with a self-assessment, and then asking for help. It changes everything about a companionship inventory. Now a companion's perspective is no longer unwelcome criticism but instead solicited advice.

Notice how the difference in giving *unwanted criticism* versus *responding to desired requests for help* in companionship inventories changes both what we say to each other and how we say it. The following table demonstrates a few examples of this:

From	To
Here's what you should do . . .	I agree with you. What can you do about it?
If only you would be more . . .	How do you think I could help you most?
No one likes it when you . . .	What do you think is the best way to assess the impact of . . . ?

When teaching this forward-looking method based on individual self-assessment for companionship inventories, some missionaries have said: "What if my companion doesn't identify things that he is really doing wrong? Shouldn't I tell him about it?" Notice the presumption of this question: "You are wrong, I'm going to correct you." Conflict and defensiveness are likely to follow. This judgmental approach is almost certain to fail every time. Companionship inventories depend on a missionary *deciding* what is important—not merely being told by a companion—and then using the companion as a "sounding board" and catalyst for improving. It honors a companion's agency without forcing opinions onto the other missionary.

Missionaries should own their own feelings and avoid projecting, labelling, or telling their companions what they should do or what's wrong with them. Do not become an amateur psychologist. Do not judge intentions or motives. Instead, let your companions tell you what they want to do better or differently or what they would like to achieve, and then offer suggestions at their invitation. When missionaries really love their companions, they listen intently, giving their companions time and space to explore their own mission-related goals and aspirations out loud with someone who truly cares about them. Sometimes, all it takes is empathetic listening to reduce the feeling of "I need to do everything on my own" and instead promote real companionability.

HOW TO AVOID UNDERMINING YOUR COMPANION

We may, at times, without realizing it, undermine our companions or other missionaries in the mission. The inclination to gossip or highlight the weaknesses of others is almost universal. One study found that about eighty percent of conversations among adults focused on someone who wasn't present.[1] Eighty percent! Talking about someone who's not part of the conversation *is* the definition of gossip—even when you think it's not bad or negative. It's the definition of "talking behind someone's back." If you would say the same thing if they were present, then do it. Wait until they are part of a conversation and then speak openly about them when they are able to participate in the conversation.

Most of us need to make an effort to avoid spreading those "juicy tidbits" that we think prop us up even as they are tearing others down. We are gossiping when we are:

- Speaking negatively of other missionaries
- Criticizing their attributes, actions, or efforts
- Sabotaging other missionaries' reputations
- Kidding on the square or making jokes at other missionaries' expense
- Pointing out and laughing at other missionaries' mistakes
- Constantly adding additional comments that show how smart you are

We read in Proverbs 26:20, "Where no wood is, there the fire goeth out: so where there is no talebearer, the strife ceaseth."

Too many missionaries gossip about each other without really knowing they are doing it. Talking about other missionaries in a negative way hurts both the speaker, and the target of unfavorable remarks. When talking about another missionary—or when someone else is talking about another missionary who is not a part of a conversation, consider this single, important question: "Why are you telling me this?"

Asking this question (of yourself or others) disrupts any self-serving motive. It's a way of calling yourself (or others) to task and considering the purpose behind a remark. If your purpose is to compliment or build someone up or use them as a positive example, go ahead and say it. On the other hand, if it plants doubts or is a negative reflection about another person, don't say it. You'll be doing yourself a favor as much as them. Instead of creating a reputation for yourself as a missionary who looks for what's wrong in others, you'll develop a reputation as a missionary who builds others up. "Talebearers," as the scriptures note, do themselves much more harm than they inflict on others. They get a reputation for gossip and others avoid them when possible. "Let no corrupt communication proceed out of your mouth," Paul wrote to the Ephesians, "but that which is good to the use of edifying, that it may minister grace unto the hearers" (Ephesians 4:29).

RESHAPING RELATIONSHIPS WITH YOUR COMPANIONS

Just as it's important to avoid these "irritators"—getting annoyed, showing disrespect, and gossiping—so it's also important to proactively seek ways to develop a positive relationship with your companion. Sometimes, it happens naturally. Most of the time, like any other relationship, you have to work at it. Having your companion's best interest at heart is a good starting point. People who are "relationship builders" treat everyone—especially the little guy—in the same positive, uplifting way that they treat others. The cashier at the grocery store, the new missionary in the zone who seems to be having a hard time adjusting, and even the mission president all get treated with the same personal attention and thoughtful regard.

Here are some pointers to get started to supplement suggestions in *Preach My Gospel* and *Adjusting to Missionary Life* which you might also want to review. All of these suggestions can help you improve a challenging companion relationship or take a good relationship to even greater heights.

UNEXPECTED ACTS

Missionaries who build great relationships don't just think about other people, they act on those thoughts. One easy way to act on your good intentions is to give *unexpected praise.* Everyone appreciates sincere, unexpected praise—it's like getting flowers not because it's Valentine's Day, but "just because." Unexpected praise helps others feel better about themselves and lets them know you're thinking about them (which, if you think about it, is flattering in itself).

Frederick Herzburg, a prominent social scientist, has suggested a simple way to give unexpected praise that lasts. He says giving unexpected praise starts by getting specific.[2] Note a specific detail that you like or admire about someone else: your companion, a store clerk, a member. Then say something like: "I'll bet doing that so well makes you feel very good. How did you learn how to do it?" Asking this follow up question lets your companion, the store clerk, or member share more about it so that they get their own "internal engine" revved up by examining what they do and explaining it to you. By doing this, they are acknowledging to themselves something they do well in addition to what you've noticed about them. This is the best kind of praise: both from within and outside.

Like giving praise, showing kindness is good for us. It makes us—the giver—feel better along with the receiver. Research shows a direct link between "random acts of kindness" and having a positive, optimistic outlook on life. Showing kindness just makes us happier people. Why do such acts of kindness increase a person's sense of happiness? One reason is that kindness promotes gratitude. Another factor is that showing kindness to others heightens our own sense of good fortune. Last, kindness promotes empathy and compassion, which in turn leads to a sense of interconnectedness with others.

Kindness can especially help those who feel depressed, isolated, or different; that is why performing acts of service is so powerful. When we feel connected with others, we lessen loneliness and stress. Such acts of service and kindness can begin at home with our companion and significantly fortify companion relations. Kindness is potent in strengthening a sense of community and belonging. Research has shown that compassion and kindness also boost our immune systems and help reduce negative emotions such as anxiety, anger, and depression, providing benefits all around.[3]

So, take a little time every day to do something nice for your companion, not because you're expected to or because you think of it as "service," but simply because you are working toward common goals. Enable your companionship to incorporate the love embodied in the gospel of Christ. Unexpected, unplanned, and unscripted acts of kindness make the world a better place and strengthen relationships between companions in remarkable ways. When you do such spontaneous little acts of kindness, all of your relationships with others will improve dramatically.

DON'T SWEAT THE SMALL STUFF

We waste our energy and too much of our lives getting upset over what are sometimes small annoyances in life. Why stress so much? "Will this matter in a year?" my mother used to say, "If not, then don't sweat the small stuff."

Richard Carlson liked that phrase too and turned it into a book: *Don't Sweat the Small Stuff.* He kept it a small book so more people would buy it without worrying about how much it costs. There are no revealing or dramatic insights in the book, just a lot of helpful reminders that life is short, and the more we can help each other out, the better. It's all about perspective, really. If our perspective about life is long-range—if we remember we are eternal beings merely passing through mortality, we realize that it's not what we achieve or acquire that matters most, but it's all about what we learn. Many of the chapter titles say it all and require no further explanation for us to "get it." Here's a few chapter titles, a few suggestions, that are also especially useful reminders for missionaries:

- Learn to Live in the Present Moment
- Let Others Be "Right" Most of the Time
- Surrender to the Fact that Life Isn't Fair
- Allow Yourself to Be Bored
- Imagine Yourself at Your Own Funeral
- Spend a Moment Every Day Thinking of Someone to Thank
- Breathe Before You Speak[4]

A mission is so much sweeter when we celebrate little victories and don't worry as much about little annoyances. President Spencer W. Kimball was fond of quoting the German poet Goethe who said: "Never let the things which matter most be at the mercy of things which matter least." We tend to get caught up in things that don't really matter as missionaries: transfers, leadership assignments, recognition. None of this matter. What matters most is setting aside our prior lifestyles and ambitions and forgetting ourselves in the service of the Lord. Can there be anything better than that?

FORGIVE AND MOVE ON

We all know that forgiving is better for us than holding grudges or insisting on being right. But it's easier said than done. While difficult, it can be learned. That's the conclusion of Dr. Frederic Luskin who has led the Stanford University Forgiveness Project and conducts workshops helping others to truly forgive someone who has hurt them.

Sometimes there's a misconception that forgiving is about giving in, or that it's letting people trample over you, Dr. Luskin notes in his workshops. But prior research suggests that's not the case. Truly forgiving and moving on is actually an incredibly powerful strength, and self-healing response to an offense. [5]

So, how can we forgive when necessary and move on with our heads held high? Here's four helpful steps.

1. *Learn mindfulness techniques for breathing deeply and developing alternative responses* to anger, regret, or distress. When thinking about an offense or action which someone may have done to hurt you, calm yourself first and reprogram your physical response to the event. Your physical body produces stress-related

tendencies to "flight or fight." Breathing deeply doesn't change the past, but it can help you get better control of your body's reactions. Then, you can begin to process the events in a different way. But before you can begin problem-solving, you must "bridle all your passions, that ye may be filled with love" (Alma 38:12).

2. *Tend and befriend.* This concept identified and developed by Shelley Taylor at UCLA emphasizes looking past differences by cultivating a relationship in the same way a gardener would by recognizing there is a time and season for everything and keeping the relationship intact even when hurt or exasperated. When asked how we should love our enemies, Elder Marion D. Hanks said it doesn't mean to have the same affection we might have toward our parents or best friend; but instead, that we recognize who they are and treat them as our Father in Heaven would.

3. *Count your blessings,* name them one by one. There is something fundamental about gratitude. It increases your capacity to forgive. It changes you by helping you notice the many good things in life and in your own particular life. It may not always reduce the hurt, pain or regret you may have about a past event, but it can help you to "right the ship" by increasing your capacity to forgive.

4. *Recognize that things don't always work out the way that you might want them to.* You may know this in your head but may need to remind yourself in your heart as well. You must frequently recognize that things are not always fair, and you may not have deserved something which occurred to you in the past. Regardless of what you go through, you can come to realize that all things are in the Lord's hands, and in His eternal plan everything can be made right. Knowing that you are not the judge may help you to forgive. He alone is empowered to judge. "Judge not, and ye shall not be judged: condemn not, and ye shall not be condemned: forgive, and ye shall be forgiven" (Luke 6:37).

5. *Change how the story is told in your own head.* Ultimately, forgiveness is a change in the story you tell yourself. Instead of a "poor me" narrative about getting wronged, you can change it to something like "look how I've grown, learned, and handled this situation better than before. Look how I've overcome adversity and learned to forgive and move on." This mindset can help you rewrite a new ending. It puts you in control of who you are, and who you are becoming. It lets you become more Christlike.

THE COMPARISON TRAP

Intuitively, we recognize that "comparisons are the thief of joy." Yet, they are as commonplace as rain. Studies show that young adults are especially prone to comparisons with others. How do I stack up? Missionaries, in particular, can get caught up in assessing their worth or contribution based on all sorts of external comparisons: baptisms, leadership positions, dinner invitations, and many other external factors. In a status-oriented world, these markers promote unhealthy competition and can ruin personal and spiritual self-esteem. While we may recognize these "natural man," tendencies, they can also be difficult to ignore.

The alternative to external comparisons—which can be grossly inaccurate and likely incomplete—is to use only ourselves and our progress toward eternal goals for comparison. For instance, cross country and marathon runners today strive to improve their own PR, their own personal record (or personal best). This is strictly an internal assessment with no external comparison.

In the book of Hebrews we read: "Wherefore seeing we also are compassed about with so great a cloud of witnesses, let us lay aside every weight, and the sin which doth so easily beset us, and let us run with patience the race that is set before us" (Hebrews 12:1).

While "the sin which doth so easily beset us" is not specifically mentioned, many Bible scholars say it is about *envy*: a feeling of resentment toward others because of their attributes or accomplishments. Envy results in a never-ending downward cycle of gossip, blame, and sarcasm. It tears others down in an attempt to bring ourselves up. Elder Jeffrey R. Holland has said that God cheers on every type of runner in every race, reminding us that the race is against sin, not against each other. Heavenly Father is, indeed, no respecter of persons and not only wants the best for each of us but amplifies the best in each of us.[6]

Elder Craig Zwick has further noted: "We live in a world that feeds on comparisons, labeling, and criticism. Instead of seeing through [another lens], we need to look inward for the godly attributes to which we each lay claim."[7]

Comparisons are never accurate—how can they be? We can never know the whole story about others or their situations. We don't know what privileges they began with, what advantages they possessed, what support they have been given, or what needs they have. The envy that comparisons breed can turn good people into sulking protestors. Take the brother of the "Prodigal son." He had everything: land, cattle, sheep, and tents. But no fatted calf. He saw what he did not have rather than what he had. As Elder Jeffrey R. Holland noted, this other son failed to see *this was not a rival returning*, it was his brother. At least momentarily, envy overruled compassion. Elder Holland notes in this important general conference address:

> It has been said that envy is the one sin to which no one readily confesses, but just how widespread that tendency can be is suggested in the old Danish proverb, "If envy were a fever, all the world would be ill." The parson in Chaucer's *Canterbury Tales* laments it because it is so far-reaching—it can resent anything, including any virtue and talent, and it can be offended by everything, including every goodness and joy. As others seem to grow larger in our sight, we think we must therefore be smaller.[8]

We can overcome this natural tendency to compare by focusing more on godly attributes and less on external markers. Missionaries are called to serve as emissaries of the Lord. They are not "called" as district or zone leaders, sister training leaders, or the like. They may be *appointed* to fill these necessary leadership roles for a time, but their only calling remains as a full-time missionary. In fact, missionaries fill these roles for many different reasons—because of what they need to learn or improve upon in many instances—and by supporting and helping them, others learn valuable lessons as well. In this regard, Elder Boyd K. Packer noted, quoting John Milton, author of *Paradise Lost*, "They also serve who only stand and wait." Or as Truman G. Madsen, once said: sometimes we are called, not to be called. Our most significant Christlike needs are met at such moments by supporting others rather than being in charge.

Sister Carol F. McConkie, First Counselor in the Young Women General Presidency, emphasized the importance of developing these Christlike attributes rather than debilitating comparisons by noting:

> In the work of salvation, there is no room for comparison, criticism, or condemnation. . . . This sacred work is about developing

a broken heart, a contrite spirit, and a willingness to use our divine gifts and unique talents to do the Lord's work in His way.[9]

SUMMARY

Relationships are a part of life. While on a mission, the strength of a relationship can make or break your success. That is why it is vital that all missionaries learn how to get along with others, especially their companions. This is a skill that can be learned, and it is done by seeking to avoid contention and focusing on building the relationship. Missionaries should learn to view their companions with greater love and avoid focusing on what they do wrong. They should focus on what they can do to improve the relationship, not on what their companion can do. Joyce Meyer said in an oft-quoted observation: "we can improve our relationships with others by leaps and bounds if we become encouragers instead of critics." In order to be as successful as possible in the mission field, seek first to be successful in your relationships.

REFERENCES

1. Rosemary Black, "Gossip Makes Up 80 Percent of Our Conversations—and That Might Be OK: Experts," *Daily News,* September 9, 2009, nydailynews.com.
2. Jim Taylor, "Parenting: Don't Praise Your Children!" *Psychology Today*, September 3, 2009, psychologytoday.com.
3. Kathleen Raven, "The Immune System & Acts of Kindness," Yale School of Medicine, fall 2018.
4. Richard Carlson, *Don't Sweat the Small Stuff . . . and It's All Small Stuff* (New York: Hachette Press, 1997).
5. Fred Luskin, *Forgive for Good* (New York: HarperOne, 2003).
6. Jeffrey R. Holland, "Laborers in the Vineyard," *Ensign*, May 2010, 31.
7. W. Craig Zwick, "Lord, Wilt Thou Cause That My Eyes May Be Opened," *Ensign*, November 2017, 98.
8. Jeffrey R. Holland, "The Other Prodigal," *Ensign,* May 2002.
9. Carol F. McConkie, "How to Serve a Righteous Cause," *Ensign*, November 2015, 13–14.

Chapter 9

RAINY DAYS AND LOCKDOWNS
DON'T NEED TO GET YOU DOWN

How to be a virtual missionary

There are times when you can't go outside and proselyte: bad weather, contentious local political elections, a companion's illness, even COVID-based lockdown requirements. The recent coronavirus pandemic disrupted millions of lives, thousands of businesses, and isolated not only missionaries but also ordinary people from each other. In many locations in the USA and abroad, missionaries were on lockdown for months. When this happens, what can you do?

In too many instances, missionaries didn't know what to do. After reading their scriptures and following up with a few investigators, they were bored with no place to go and seemingly nothing to do. Some became discouraged. Some even returned home.

But not everywhere. In locations where missionaries were used to remaining indoors for extended periods of time, they swung into action with contingency plans they had developed when faced with conditions requiring them to remain indoors. Mardi Gras in New Orleans, snowstorms in Montana, and elections in many Latin American countries can make proselyting difficult, if not impossible for a few days or a few weeks. Even a companion with a cold or flu can stymie traditional proselyting for days, and force you to come up with alternative plans. It happens everywhere and often enough that creating alternative plans should really become part of every missionary's regime. You should always have a Plan B ready to implement when things don't go as expected.

CONFINEMENT PLANS

During the recent COVID-19 outbreak, missionaries were confined to their apartments in some cases for months. Armed police patrolled the streets in places like Baltimore, Chicago, and New York ensuring that people remained indoors, and normal activities were curtailed in churches, restaurants, and parks. But such restrictions don't have to get you down. Instead, use them to your advantage. Here's how.

In studies about people who are confined for extended periods—in space, in the military, in the Antarctic—researchers have described some important tips and key activities that should occur which we will review in the following sections. As missionaries, you can learn much from these types of experiences, and apply them when confined to an apartment for extended periods of time. Here's what others have found helpful when confined or isolated and unable to do things they way they would like to do them. You can put them into practice yourself when you are restricted and must remain indoors.

- *Develop a schedule and stick to it*: routines help us in so many ways. Schedules keep us going. They give us structure. They take our minds off other things. Keep up the prescribed missionary schedule including standard times for personal and companion study, planning, and contacting. Okay, maybe it will be a different kind of proselyting during a pandemic or thunderstorm or holiday celebration, but you can be proselyting nearly the same with available technological tools and members.
- *Dress for the day in standard missionary attire:* there is scientific data that suggests how we dress affects our moods, attitudes, and demeanor. Experiments with different groups of people show we are more conscious of our duties and pay more attention if we dress appropriately for daily tasks even if there are long periods of "down time" during the day. For instance,

putting on a sports uniform makes you ready to play ball. In experimental tests, just putting on a lab coat noticeably caused people to pay more attention and make fewer mistakes.[1] Dressing in missionary attire will help you feel, think, and behave more like a missionary throughout the day. Even if you are confined to your apartment with only your companion, dress everyday as if you are planning to meet your mission president.

- *Set reachable goals for each day:* whether it's practicing the piano, trying a new recipe, or exercising, set reachable goals on a daily basis. Then, at the end of the day, assess how well you've done. These bite size goals will keep you going, help you stay focused, and provide the kind of motivational "juice" that will help you not only stay engaged in your missionary efforts, but also remain as productive as possible.

- *Do something fun throughout the day:* eat a delicious snack or play catch with a nerf ball with your companion, for instance. Whatever it is that you enjoy—while keeping mission rules— find ways to take a break, and do it for a few minutes throughout the day. There are plenty of fun activities that can ease each day during long periods of confinement such as drawing caricatures, baking a cake, or playing a board game.

- *Call or write a friend:* we feel less isolated if we are able to connect with friends—even a made up friend. In the movie *Cast Away*, Tom Hanks plays a FedEx employee whose plane crashes, and he eventually ends up on a deserted island in the Pacific Ocean. Isolated and confined to the island, he must learn to fend for himself. Eventually, he turns a volleyball—made by the Wilson company—into "a friend." Talking to the friend keeps him going year after year until he eventually builds a raft and leaves the island. When he leaves the island after being on it for four and a half years, he takes "Wilson"—the volleyball— with him. They had a connection, a shared bond, and Hanks's character refuses to leave the volleyball behind when he leaves. Talking to friends or even members when possible, can keep us from feeling lonely during isolation and can keep us motivated.

- *Take mental inventory of your well-being:* you can do this throughout the day just by checking your attitude. You can find those things that you are grateful for, and mentally remind yourself of the good things you enjoy. Celebrate them! "Go thy way, eat thy bread with joy . . ." (Ecclesiastes 9:7). Become a "list maker" and make a daily written inventory of your blessings and look at it regularly.

- ***Reframe the situation:*** Scott Kelly, an American astronaut who spent 340 days confined in space, said that what helped him avoid "cabin fever" was focusing on what he *could* do rather than what he was *unable* to do. He redefined what was possible and unique about being confined in space, and then let his imagination and creativity take over. For instance, he counted the days until he was able to take a space walk despite mundane tasks that he repeated day after day preparing for it. He made daily observations about ordinary activities and described the uniqueness of them, despite what he would have originally considered as simply routine and ordinary activities. He made a game out of doing regular activities and measured his speed or capability in doing them. Changing his point of view to what he *could* do rather than what he was *prevented* from doing and making games out of ordinary tasks made a huge difference in his own attitude.[2]

When you are confined to your apartment because of weather, a companion's illness, a pandemic, or other factors, you can reframe your situation by asking:

- What is unique about being confined to my apartment today?
- What opportunities does it give me to do things differently?

There's always something productive you can do, and usually you can make a game out of doing it as well. In fact, making a game out of times when you can't get outside is a great option. But don't just pass the time; make the most of it. Turn restrictions into an incentive to find creative ways do missionary service. You can do this by phone contacting, discovering groups on social media that share common interest with you, preparing for open houses, baking for others, and many other innovative ways to become better acquainted with others in the area and serve them.

PHONE CONTACTING

Missionary service is never easy, and it has its own innate challenges under the best of circumstances. When confined to your apartment due to weather, a companion's illness, or outside disruptions you can continue to teach and follow up with current investigators, recent converts, and both less-active and active members over the phone. It does, however, take a little imagination and ingenuity to really connect with people over the phone. But it can be done, and it can produce amazing results. Here's an example from a missionary who consistently did phone contacting while quarantined during the coronavirus pandemic:

> I had very little success during the first 6 months of my mission. We knocked on lots of doors, we taught English classes, we visited with members seeking referrals with very few positive results. I became very discouraged and often wondered if I was ever going to do any good at all on my mission or if my mission was simply going to be a "study abroad" experience for 2 years. Then, the coronavirus hit. We had to stay inside. We had one investigator that we had started teaching before the lockdown that we continued to teach over the phone. When we talked with him, we didn't just ask how he was doing or just talk about the lessons. We got to know him in ways that we hadn't before. We became each other's life lines to the outside world. There were fewer distractions than normal because we all had to listen carefully to get what each other was saying. It was one of the best teaching experiences of my mission. And when he was baptized, it made it even sweeter.

There's no substitute for genuine interest in others. You can't fake it, but you *can* learn it. The key for developing an interest in others is to ask questions *without an agenda*. Most people who make phone calls or knock on doors have an angle. They want us to do something or buy something. Sometimes missionaries get caught up in that as well. They focus on numbers or baptisms. But when you eliminate those tendencies and instead focus on others—their interests and their words—wonderful conversations happen. Conversations can get started as easily over the phone as it can face-to-face—by finding out about others interests rather than simply delivering your message.

HOW TO GET STARTED

During the coronavirus pandemic, missionaries in many different locations decided to contact organizations that might welcome those who were new to the area. Local missionaries contacted libraries, sports clubs, newcomers groups, book clubs, music and theatrical groups, and others with websites or Facebook pages in their area. They visited these sites on their p-day and wrote down phone numbers for anyone listed. Then, they called these contacts during the week and introduced themselves. Since they were new in the area, they asked about what these groups could offer someone like them. Then, they explained why they were new and waited to see if this person would ask more about the Church. In other cases, these missionaries contacted local groups based on their own personal interests in music, reading, sports, baking, historical sites, and the like.

Greetings are critical. How you introduce yourself and what you say in the first ten to fifteen seconds likely makes the difference between the person staying on the line or hanging up. Don't be vague, be direct and say who you are. Then, state your purpose in calling is not to talk about the Church, but to get to know more about their organization and see if there is any service they could offer.

There is no single *right way* to get started when introducing yourself, but there are several wrong ways. Your words are not the only things that matter here. Your intentions, your sincerity, and your tone of voice will all come through loud and clear even when the phone connection is bad. Keep that in mind when calling. Here are some examples of creative approaches various missionaries have used after introducing themselves over the phone:

- "We're calling because we're interested in libraries in the area and wonder if you would tell us about your library."
- "We're looking for ways to serve the community/neighborhood and wonder what we could do for you or your neighbors."

- "We're new in the area and have been asked to learn more about local customs. Could you take a few minutes to visit with us?"
- "People have been kind to us lately and we are interested in 'paying it forward' with 'random acts of kindness.' Do you know someone who needs cheering up that we could call or serve?"
- "We are new to the area and are interested in learning more about it from local residents. Could you take a few minutes to share your thoughts about living here?"

In research done by Stanford University on the types of requests strangers are most likely to respond to (whether in person, on the phone, or online) there are three significant factors that determine whether or not someone will stop and listen—or simply hang up the phone, ignore a text message, or avoid a Facebook post. These are:

1. **the sincerity of the requestor,**
2. **a clear need in a request, and**
3. **information (or help) that can be readily provided.**[3]

Developing a sincere yet unique approach requires imagination and experimentation. Start by focusing on the needs of others as soon as possible. Get acquainted right away, get personal, and show that your primary purpose is to learn about them, share a common interest, or to be helpful in some way rather than merely pursue a predetermined agenda. For instance, one missionary said that during the COVID-19 lockdown some of his best phone contacting experiences came when he quickly found a topic of common interest. During that period, he talked with several less-active members and others about their mutual disappointment over the cancellation of the NCAA Men's basketball tournament. With this common ground established, they were then able to have meaningful gospel discussions. He shared these additional insights about a particular phone conversation:

> I remember talking to one guy who had not been to church for years. The conversation drifted to March Madness and how disappointed I was that it was cancelled. He got very excited on the phone and talked about how it was the one time of the year he connected with some old high school buddies in making

predictions. We had several follow up phone visits where I was able to share more gospel oriented messages, but it all started with a shared interest in talking about college basketball.

Elder Dieter. F Uchtdorf recently spoke in general conference about ways that we can serve as missionaries through such normal and natural conversations that can lead to a gospel discussion whether on the phone, online, or in person.

I am not asking that you stand on a street corner with a megaphone and shout out Book of Mormon verses. What I am asking is that you always look for opportunities to bring up your faith in natural and normal ways with people—both in person as well as online. I am asking that you "stand as witnesses" of the power of the gospel at all times—and when necessary, use words.

Elder Uchtdorf goes on to emphasize "There are many normal and natural ways to do this, from daily acts of kindness to personal testimonials on YouTube, Facebook, Instagram, or Twitter to simple conversations with people you meet." [4] This applies equally to full-time missionaries as well as ordinary members. Developing the right hook requires imagination and experimentation. But remember, focus on the needs of others as soon as possible. Get acquainted right away, get personal, and show that your primary purpose is to learn and be helpful, not merely to achieve a quota.

Elder Oaks discussed the importance of finding out about others interests and establishing common ground when he spoke about how to share the gospel.

They may also be interested when they are seeking more happiness, closeness to God, or a better understanding of the purpose of life. Therefore, we must carefully and prayerfully seek discernment on how to inquire about others' interest to learn more. This will depend on various things, such as another person's current circumstances and our relationship with him or her. [5]

Practice, experimentation, genuineness, and the Spirit will help any missionary have strong gospel conversations during phone contacting.

When missionaries decide their primary purpose is to "share the gospel" and not merely to baptize investigators, everything changes. We share the gospel by the little things we do, the kind words we offer to strangers, the help we give in the community, and the person we cheer up who is sad or lonely or uncertain.

As the Savior taught in Matthew 25:34–35:

> Then shall the King say unto them on his right hand, Come, ye blessed of my Father, inherit the kingdom prepared for you from the foundation of the world: For I was an hungred, and ye gave me meat: I was thirsty, and ye gave me drink: I was a stranger, and ye took me in.

There are gospel lessons that will never be forgotten when accompanied by the power of the Holy Ghost regardless of whether someone chooses to join the Church. The Spirit can be felt even through a phone contact.

WHO TO CALL

Unsolicited phone calls to complete strangers are rarely effective. A better approach is to develop a phone plan that includes local organizations, investigators, recent converts, less-active members, active members, ward leaders, and neighborhood service providers. A customized plan with a focus on *their interests*, not *your interests,* as Elder Oaks advocates, is the best approach for you to have many positive gospel discussions.

When Larry Scott was a missionary, he used this kind of purposeful "understand their interests first" approach when he and his companion had used all their allotted driving miles and were forced to stop driving. Their proselyting area was very spread out, so they spent some time calling members and others for referrals and suggestions on who to contact. He writes this about his experience:

> We were contacting people by phone, and I was given a referral to contact Claire Bernice Smith. I called her on the phone and we just visited for a while. Then, she asked why I was serving a

mission. She was interested! Later, after several weeks of teaching her, she was baptized. It was one of the greatest experiences of my mission.

People will respond on the phone in much the same way as they will likely respond in person. Getting started with cheerful and unique greetings, developing a rapport, and asking for help they can give will enable missionaries to have many more gospel conversations than if they merely go through the motions. Consider each group—active members, less-active members, or current investigators—and then ask yourself:

- What will their initial reactions likely be to my call?
- How can I minimize or dispel any concerns about my purpose?
- What questions can I ask to learn more about their interests or needs?
- What can I say about my own background that might interest them?
- How can I transition to a gospel conversation?

FOLLOW UP WITH LESS-ACTIVE MEMBERS

Worldwide, missionaries have been encouraged to reach out to less-active members. Regardless of bad weather or unusual circumstances where you may need to remain in your apartment, get the names of three to five less-active members each week from ward or branch leaders. Get a little background on each of them and suggestions for the best way to approach them from the ward or branch leaders as well. Phone contacting can be especially helpful with these less-active members. Call and inquire about them, their family, and their circumstances. Offer to help or serve in some way. Ask if you can schedule a short discussion with family members over the phone; then give a ten to fifteen minute lesson from *Preach My Gospel*. Find out what topics are of most interest. Next, tell them about related resources on the internet, especially at the Church's website. Share your testimony. Extend an invitation to act. Schedule another phone appointment a few days later.

A similar approach can be taken with each group of members, investigators, or even community leaders:

- Get acquainted personally by "dropping the curtain" that may exist between you and them; share a bit of your own personal background and become friends rather than remaining strangers.
- Determine some of their personal needs and interests from their perspective, not yours.
- Offer to help or serve in some way. Even if you can't leave your apartment there are things you can organize, prepare, or coordinate with the assistance of others.
- Give feedback when someone makes a suggestion or gives a referral. Get back to them later and let them know what happened.
- Be persistent and patient. You may need to try various approaches or call back often to make a connection or even get ahold of individuals in the first place.
- Handle rejection without taking it personally—it's not about you—it is Heavenly Father's work, and we are merely His agents.

While phone contacting can be effective, there are a wide variety of other activities you can participate in when you are confined to your apartment. They take a little creativity, but with suggestions from ward or branch leaders, they can also be helpful. Here are some examples from missionaries around the world who made the most of their time when they could not go outside to proselyte.

CONTACT INTEREST GROUPS ON THE INTERNET

We all have unique personal interests. Maybe before your mission you were a runner, a musician, a cook, a snowboarder. So what's the easiest thing in the world to talk about? Things that interest you, right? Whatever your interests, hobbies, or pastimes, there are groups on social media or the internet that have similar interests as you. Find them and introduce yourself simply by talking about your common interests. It's the kind of fellowshipping you may be encouraging Church members to do already. You can do it as well using Wi-Fi at the Church when you can't do standard proselyting.

Get started by making your own list of personal interests and hobbies. Think broadly about anything and everything you are interested in from gardening and photography to fishing and travel; from camping and music to singing and geocaching. The longer the list you make the better.

Next, look for groups with similar interests on social media and the Internet. Read about them. Look at their calendar and recent activities. If there are contact names, call them. If there are discussions threads on topics of interest to you, join in and comment on them. Let your own interests be your guide. Give your thoughts on whatever is being discussed or planned to recently has been recently completed. Share similar experiences or offer your own insights. When others ask about your background, tell them. But start simply by commenting on the topic that is under discussion. Let others see your common interests, and sooner or later they will ask about what you are doing in the area and why you are doing it.

Here's an example of how a full-time sister missionary used her interest in jazz music to contact others with similar interests. Before her mission, she played both the piano and clarinet with two different performing groups in her hometown. While on lockdown due to the COVID-19 pandemic, she found a local radio station's website featuring jazz music. She joined in several conversation threads, commenting about various artists and offering observations about their music. Because of her insights, others asked about her background. This gave her an opportunity not only to tell about her musical training but also about her mission and assignment in the local area. For several people, it was eye-opening that someone could be both a music aficionado and a committed member of the Church. They had the previous impression that Church members were dull and straitlaced and uninterested in contemporary jazz music. After dispelling common stereotypes, she and her companion were able to have several missionary discussions on Zoom and even attendance at church for these newly found investigators.

There are likely many different types of interest groups that you could contact regardless of your location. Look for local groups on social media and the Internet. Since all missionaries are more or less new to any area, it is an easy way to get acquainted. Ask for suggestions from members on local sites to visit. Get acquainted on those sites first before giving a gospel message. If you make enough interesting comments, you will have many opportunities for follow up gospel discussions. This is a unique way to reach people virtually who may be reluctant to open their door when you knock on it, but may open their hearts to the Holy Ghost if you first let them see who you are and that you are just an ordinary person with an extraordinary message.

WRITE COLORFUL WARD/BRANCH HISTORIES

Write a history of the ward/branch and the town where you live. Think about the legacy that you will be leaving! You can enlist the help of longtime residents as well as Family History specialists. You don't have to be an accomplished writer, just an interested observer and interviewer. Focus on how the ward/branch began and the testimonies of those who were early members. Tell stories about challenges they faced and obstacles they overcame in their faith, their professions, their families, and the community.

Call branch members and ask for events that are part of the history of the Branch. Record what they say on your phone (if you have that capability), and transcribe it later. Try to focus on several different interesting incidents and how people remember them. Think of it as making your own version of *Fiddler on the Roof* with interesting characters and ordinary incidents that nonetheless are funny or sad or clever or poignant. Tell inspiring stories of faith and perseverance just like family history specialists do for their own family histories.

You don't have to be a journalist to write a ward or branch history, and you don't have to do this alone. Engage other missionaries in your district or members of the ward or branch who are interested in this history of the Church in the area. Use outside resources at the library or others who are familiar with the area and know something about the growth of the Church in the area.

CONSTRUCT STREET DISPLAYS

Make Church displays and put them on the street in front of your apartment with your contact information and slices of baked goods such as banana bread to entice passers to stop by and take a look. When you are not able to have Church open houses, this is a way to take an "open house" to a nearby community. It's like a mobile Church "Visitors Center" with displays, pamphlets, and explanations. These can be unattended with contact information on an easel or table—such as when missionaries were on lockdown during COVID-19—or they can be eye-catching displays staffed by members when as missionaries you are confined to your apartment.

Your street displays are like billboards for retail stores. If you want to get noticed, avoid the predictable. Use colorful and enticing images that fit your locale. Many churches use outside signage with Bible quotes or whimsical, clever sayings. Discuss locations, display boards, and needed support with ward members and ward missionaries. Effective displays don't need to be expensive, but they do need to look professional. You can use members to help you create visually appealing displays to supplement standard Church posters and exhibits.

CREATE ENTERTAINING VIDEOS FOR LOCAL UNITS

There are several ways to tell a story or convey a message. You can speak it, you can draw it, you can write it, or you can show it. Visual storytelling— the kind that is faith promoting and memorable—doesn't take expensive equipment or years of experience. It just takes a little time, patience, and ingenuity. Even using the video feature on a smartphone can help capture and create an inspiring story. Elder Neil L. Andersen even used a homemade video once to supplement his general conference talk, showing that it doesn't take sophisticated photography skills or equipment to put together a short and effective video that can be posted on social media or used in other ways.

Creating one to three minute videos that are similar to the "I am a Mormon" campaign that the Church produced a few years back can be both fun for missionaries, and another way to share the gospel. Check out the Church's website for inspiration and other ideas. Ask members in the ward or branch who have smartphones to make these short videos, and send them to their friends and to you. Another idea is to have them use Marco Polo and ask them to invite their friends (and you) to view them. Make these videos interactive by asking for comments and questions, and sharing inspiring, faith-promoting stories.

MAKE A TREAT

In many cultures, food is an expression of admiration, care, and support. When words fail—such as following the passing of a loved one—food can fill the gap. Making a casserole, a pie, or a treat communicates our desire to connect and relate when words themselves are inadequate. Baking and sharing what we've made with others is increasingly getting attention for the benefits it gives to us, as well as for those with whom we share what we have made. For instance, John Waite, who won the *Great British Bake Off* in 2012, said that baking was a significant help in managing his depression and sadness.[6]

Baking requires thinking things through step-by-step and following specific directions in a recipe to get it right. By following specific instructions, we are less likely to be overwhelmed by outside events or feelings of sadness, less likely to stress about "what might have been" or "what could have been" and instead stay in the "here and now."

Known as "behavioral activation therapy," baking has been shown to reduce anxiety—especially when dealing with uncertain events or activities—and thereby enhance the overall well-being of the *giver.*[7] Such ordinary activities—baking, drawing, sewing, or making crafts—also can give us a feeling of accomplishment; we have tangible evidence that we have accomplished something. When a gift is given, it also helps us feel the benefits of generosity and service. We benefit emotionally when we do something tangible for others.

Baking can be therapeutic as well as show others that we are thinking about them and are interested in brightening their day or lightening their load of responsibilities.

So make and take cookies or cake and leave it on the doorstep (if necessary) for anyone who needs some cheering up. Send a text or leave a note as you leave, so they will know that you've thought of them and the treat you've left on their doorstep is from you. "Food is love," the Italians say. Though it may be only one way to communicate generosity, acceptance, and admiration, it does seem to be an important way of doing so. Making a treat and taking it to others—even if you don't deliver it in person—is a universal way of expressing appreciation.

SUMMARY

When your proselyting routine is disrupted and you must stay in your apartment, look for creative alternatives to share the gospel that still lets you fulfill your calling. There's almost no limit to imaginative ways to call, write, post, create, build, and bake your way to gospel conversations. When being "apartment bound" for an extended period, look for ways to "tend and befriend" by both connecting more with family and friends, and others in the community. Work to find creative ways of doing things for others. *Tending and befriending* can reduce your own stress and feelings of boredom as well as channel your energies toward productive outcomes. The worst thing you can do is simply sit around and wait for whatever is keeping you in your apartment to pass. Like the Tom Hanks character in *Cast Away*, we may not be able to control everything, but we can be proactive and improvise and refuse to be overwhelmed by events—big or small.

REFERENCES

1. Caroline Adams Miller and Michael B. Frisch, *Creating Your Best Life Now: The Ultimate Life List Guide* (New York: Sterling), 147–149.
2. Scott Kelly, "I Spent a Year in Space, and I Have Tips on Isolation to Share," *New York Times,* March 21, 2020, nytimes.com.
3. "The Science Of Influence: How to Persuade Others and Hold Their Attention," *Think Fast, Talk Smart: The Podcast,* hosted by Matt Abrahams with guest Zakary Tormala at Stanford Graduate School of Business, May 26, 2020, gsb.stanford.edu/insights/science-influence-how-persuade-others-hold-their-attention.
4. Dieter F. Uchtdorf "Sharing What Is In Your Heart," *Ensign*, May 2019, 17.
5. Dallin H. Oaks "Sharing the Restored Gospel," *Ensign*, November 2016, 59.
6. Claire Spreadbury, "John Whaite: Baking is Self-Care to Me," *Irish News,* October 19, 2019, irishnews.com/lifestyle/2019/10/19/news/john-whaite-baking-is-self-care-to-me-says-former-bake-off-winner-1734585/.
7. Jeanne Whalen, "A Road to Mental Health Through the Kitchen," *Wall Street Journal,* December 8, 2014, 11, available online at wsj.com/articles/a-road-to-mental-health-through-the-kitchen-1418059204.

Chapter 10

CONNECTING THE DOTS

How to be a complete missionary

Many things depend on how we look at them. How many squares do you see in the puzzle below?

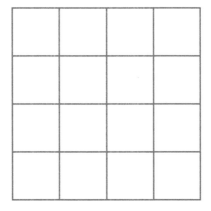

How many squares did you count? Some people see only the sixteen small squares. Others look beyond what is at first very noticeable and see 2 by 2 sets (or 4) of these smaller squares (there are 9 different sets of them). Still others see additional sets of these smaller squares: 3 by 3 sets (or 9) of these smaller squares. The outside perimeter of these 16 smaller squares is also a large square. This makes a total of 30 squares. Perspective matters.

When missionary work is seen as the quintessential work of salvation, suddenly everything changes. There's no longer any drudgery. And rejection suddenly doesn't matter either. It's never been just about you, the missionary. It's always about the service you render, the capacity for love you develop, and the lifelong commitment to living gospel principles that gets embedded in your everyday life.

Elder Jeffery R. Holland has remarked:

> It [missionary work] is by definition the most important thing you can do in the world, in time or eternity. For this reason you are engaged in the saving of the human soul. And that is the highest and holiest work in the universe. That is the thing that God Himself said was His work and glory. It is the purpose for which the Savior came to the earth and gave His life and was resurrected to open those possibilities and promises of Eternal Life. It is the purpose for which every prophet has lived, and every apostle has spoken. It is the purpose for which every missionary since Adam and Eve has gone forth to declare the truth. You join those ranks! You join that brotherhood and sisterhood, and it is as I said by definition, by theology, it is the most important thing you can do.[1]

BE THE BOOK OF MORMON
YOU WANT OTHERS TO READ

While serving as the mission president in the Ghana Accra West Mission, I recall interviewing a missionary who was discouraged. Nothing I said seemed to help. Every suggestion that I offered was met with an excuse, an explanation, a reason why the suggestion wouldn't work for him. Inspired, I finally said, "Be the Book of Mormon that you want others to read."

"What?" he replied. "What do you mean?"

"Do you believe in the Book of Mormon?" I asked. "Do you believe that it is the word of God and that a person can get nearer to God by abiding by its precepts than by any other book?"

"Yes," he said. "But what if people won't listen to me?" he replied.

"Then, be the Book of Mormon that you want people to read," I said. "Be the person who lives the Book of Mormon's message so completely that looking at you will entice others to want to know more about who you are and why this book is so important in your life. Be the Book of Mormon that you want others to read."

This is not a pithy self-help message. There is no guarantee that others will notice or care about who we are or what we are about. But our Father in Heaven will notice and, after all, isn't that all that really matters? If we have His approval, His approbation, and His confirmation that the things we are doing are pleasing to Him, is there anything else that really compares?

Collective action matters, too. We do not act alone. We are, as the song goes, "as the army of Helaman." An army that is committed to gospel principles, not merely hand-to-hand combat with naysayers.

Mahatma Gandhi once said, "If we could change ourselves, the tendencies in the world would also change. As a man changes his own nature, so does the attitude of the world change towards him . . . We need not wait to see what others do."[2]

But can we really change who we are—or are our personalities fixed by a certain age? Research today has shown that our personalities are much more elastic than was once previously thought. In fact, our personalities shift over time based on experience and intentional pursuit of various goals.

According to a recent landmark study in the *Journal of Personality and Social Psychology*, how outgoing we are, our openness to new experiences, our anxieties, our inclination toward generosity, and our ability to handle tasks and organize skills—the so-called "Big Five" personality traits—can and do change over time. These changes are based upon significant emotional events ranging from mission experiences to marriage to children and career experiences. We might not change the world, but we can change ourselves, and thereby change our place in the world.[3]

What does it take? Start with this: Be the Book of Mormon you want others to read. Ponder it. Apply it. Live it.

Preach My Gospel has many important messages. Among them is that by raising our spiritual expectations of ourselves, both our desire and our effectiveness increases. We grow spiritually as we aspire higher, believe deeper, and nurture our faith more.

A GRATEFUL HEART,
A MAGNET FOR MIRACLES

We are often told, "stop feeling sorry for yourself." While it can be hard to avoid self-pity entirely when teaching the gospel and facing rejection daily, committed missionaries choose to *exchange* self-pity for *gratitude*. Whether you write a few sentences in a gratitude journal or simply take a moment to silently acknowledge all that you have, giving thanks can transform your life. It is not just about saying the words, but what matters most is living by them.

There are various proven benefits from feeling and expressing gratitude. To begin, gratitude opens the door to more relationships. According to a 2014 study published in *Emotion*—a scientific journal—not only is saying "thank you" good manners but demonstrating appreciation can help you develop new relationships with others. The study found that even thanking people that you meet casually makes them more likely to seek an ongoing relationship.[4] So when you see a stranger is not interested at that moment in your message, thank them for listening to you, or thank someone on the street who has given you directions. Expressing gratitude can open new doors in the future; it can become the basis for gospel discussions for you or other missionaries. We are always planting seeds.

According to a 2012 study, gratitude improves physical and psychological health. Grateful people experience fewer aches and pains and report feeling healthier than other people. Gratitude also reduces a variety of toxic emotions from resentment to frustration and regret. Robert Emmons, a leading gratitude researcher, has conducted multiple studies on the link between gratitude and well-being. His research confirms that gratitude effectively increases happiness and reduces anxiety and depression.[4]

Gratitude improves self-esteem. A 2014 study published in the *Journal of Applied Sport Psychology* found that gratitude increased athletes' self-esteem, an essential component to optimal performance. Other studies have shown that gratitude reduces social comparisons.[4] Rather than becoming resentful toward other missionaries' success—a major factor in reduced self-esteem—grateful missionaries are able to appreciate others' accomplishments. While *Preach My Gospel* doesn't identify gratitude as the driving force that helps us avoid comparisons, it is very clear that comparing our success to the success of other missionaries is unhealthy and should be avoided.

For years, research has shown gratitude not only reduces stress but also promotes resilience: it helps us roll with the punches regardless of what happens to us. It promotes mental toughness. A 2003 study in the *Journal of Personality and Social Psychology* found that gratitude was a major contributor to recovery for families affected by the September 11 terrorist attacks on the World Trade Center.[4] Recognizing all that we have to be thankful for—even during the worst of times—fosters resilience among us as missionaries.

We all have the ability to cultivate more gratitude in our lives. It is a dynamic, not a static tendency. Rather than complain about the things which we think we deserve, focusing on the things we have will enable us to feel better and perform more effectively regardless of our circumstances.

DISCIPLESHIP EMBODIES DISCIPLINE

Sometimes missionaries struggle with rules: either by loosely following them, or alternately by rigidly keeping them. Neither extreme is helpful, and each can be harmful. Missionary rules are for our own benefit and protection. Loosely following mission rules can make us slothful and cause us to fail to inherit the promises offered to the obedient as promised in Hebrews 6:12:

> That ye be not slothful, but followers of them who through faith and patience inherit the promises.

On the other hand, rigidly keeping mission rules without seeing their higher purpose can promote undesirable perfectionism and unnecessary anxiety. Daniel Judd, former mission president and now dean of BYU's

Department of Religious Education, has conducted compelling research among Church members showing that legalistic beliefs and rigid adherence to rules is associated with lower mental health, higher incidences of depression, a lower sense of compassion, and an inability to feel the relief that comes from grace and repentance.[5]

Sometimes we get stuck. Sometimes we may even regress. We may swing from side to side, either for considering mission rules, an elastic band, or a rigid straitjacket. When that happens, how do we get "unstuck?" How—like being the conductor of a train—do we start moving down the right track of committed discipleship and avoid extremes in our thinking or actions?

Elder Dallin H. Oaks offers this helpful insight:

From such teachings we conclude that the Final Judgement is not just an evaluation of a sum total of good and evil acts—what we have *done*. It is an acknowledgment of the final effect of our acts and thoughts—what we have *become*. It is not enough for anyone just to go through the motions. The commandments, ordinances, and covenants of the gospel are not a list of deposits to be made in some heavenly account. The gospel of Jesus Christ is a plan that shows us how to become what our Heavenly Father desires us to become.[6]

This "power to become" is much more than "a list of deposits to be made in some heavenly account," but instead is a measure of our willingness to sacrifice whatever it takes to serve the Lord with all of our heart, might, mind, and strength. No external person or activity can measure this commitment. It flows directly from our hearts.

Elder Robert D. Hales emphasized this further in an April 2017 general conference address:

Many people hear the word *disciple* and think it means only "follower." But genuine discipleship is a state of being. This suggests more than studying and applying an individual list of attributes. Disciples live so that the characteristics of Christ are woven into the fiber of their beings, as into a spiritual tapestry.[7]

We may recognize that developing Christlike attributes and the commitment of discipleship takes time, effort, and perseverance. We may also feel inclined to think that it can always be done "later," but "later" rarely ever comes, and the time to commit to steady discipleship is now. There is great peril in procrastination.

In the scriptures, the importance of urgency is often stressed, here are some examples:

> Alma 5:31: "And the time is at hand that he must repent or he cannot be saved!"

> Alma 34:33: "I beseech of you that ye do not procrastinate the day of your repentance."

> 2 Corinthians 6:2: "Behold, now is the day of salvation."

> Doctrine and Covenants 64:25: "Ye will labor while it is called today."

The Savior also stressed the urgency of acting "now" and not waiting until "later" when a disciple approached him and asked for time to bury his father. The scriptures record: "But Jesus said unto him, Follow me; and let the dead bury their dead" (Matthew 8:22). In all likelihood, the use of the word "dead" in this verse is more accurately translated as "town" suggesting that the disciple should let the townspeople or other close relatives in the town bury his father.[8]

Like other passages, the Savior is stressing the urgency of acting now in our discipleship and avoiding procrastination. When we consider the things, we want to achieve as missionaries, they will never happen by themselves, and they likely won't happen overnight. While visualization can help, there is no substitute for simply getting started and actually doing.

Want to improve your discipleship? Start now. Identify actions you can take to increase your generosity, show gratitude, and become more committed. *Preach My Gospel* has an entire chapter on "How Do I Develop Christlike Attributes?" which can become an important place either to begin or continue your journey on the covenant path toward committed discipleship.

WALKING ON THE
ROAD TO EMMAUS

Missionaries do a lot of walking. You'll walk miles and miles each day while proselyting, contacting, visiting members, and teaching lessons. It is one of the standard activities which all missionaries do. Walking is good for you physically—you may even have a Fitbit that buzzes and acknowledges when you take ten thousand steps in a day—and it maintains missionaries physically active throughout the day. Additionally, walking is also good for you spiritually. It gives you time and space to think, reflect, and plan.

The word "walk" is mentioned more than five hundred times in the scriptures as both a metaphor and a purposeful activity, such as "walk humbly with God," "walk in the strait path," and "walking in holiness before the Lord," in addition to times when an angel walked with a prophet or Jesus walked and talked with His disciples. The spiritual, mental, and physical benefits of walking are enormous. A Stanford University study found that walking increases our creative output by more than sixty percent. According to the study "walking opens up the free flow of ideas, and it is a simple and robust solution for increasing physical and mental acuity."[9]

Missionaries spend lots of time walking. It's an "occupational characteristic," and it is a really good way to stand out as a kind of "moving billboard." It is an easy way to get noticed, to meet people, and to visibly represent the Church. It is also a way to draw closer to our Heavenly Father and our Savior.

After the Savior's crucifixion and resurrection, we read in Luke 24 that Jerusalem was all abuzz with the news. Who had heard of the events? Were they real? What does it mean? Two disciples were walking from Jerusalem to Emmaus talking about it. As they traveled, Jesus joined them, but their eyes were restrained, and they did not recognize him. As they walked, he said to them: "What manner of communication are these that ye have one to another, as ye walk, and are sad?"

The story of the disciples on the road to Emmaus is important for many reasons. It shows how Old Testament prophecies were fulfilled as well as giving additional evidence of His resurrection. But it also shows the benefits of walking and talking about the Savior in our everyday activities and how unnamed disciples can have Him join them and give them additional insights as they are able to be undistracted walking along a roadside together.

SUMMARY

Becoming a complete missionary involves hard work, diligent study, thoughtful prayer, and the Spirit of the Lord. We cannot do it alone, and the Lord needs us to do this great work. We are His ambassadors, and we are instruments in His hands. When we are worthy and committed to serving for all of the right reasons, it is evident to everyone we meet. Elder M. Russell Ballard describes a complete missionary this way:

> You know, oftentimes I'll ask new converts when they know for the first time that the Church is true. It is not unusual for them to say, "I came to know the Church is true when I was taught by the elders or sisters and felt the power of their belief and saw the radiance of their countenance." If you're not actively and anxiously engaged, the Spirit won't be empowering your missionary service as it will if you are.[10]

Who we are and why we serve—our motivation, our attitude, our commitment, our desire—matters enormously. In fact, it changes the entire course of our mission and the experiences we will get out of it.

REFERENCES

1. Jeffrey R. Holland, "Miracle of a Mission," Missionary Training Center address, 2013.
2. Mohandas K. Gandhi and Krishna Kripalani, *All Men Are Brothers* (Ahmedabad: Navajivan, 1995), 133.
3. Nathan W. Hudson and R. Chris Fraley, "Volitional Personality Trait Change: Can People Choose to Change their Personality Traits?" *Journal of Personality and Social Psychology* 109, no. 3 (2015): 490–507.

4.   Amy Morin, "Seven Scientifically Proven Benefits of Gratitude," *Psychology Today,* April 3, 2015, psychologytoday.com.

5.   Daniel K. Judd and W. Justin Dyer, "Grace, Legalism, and Mental Health Among the Latter-day Saints," *BYU Studies* vol. 59, no. 1 (2020), 4–23.

6.   Dallin H. Oaks, "The Challenge to Become," *Ensign,* November 2000.

7.   Robert D. Hales, "Becoming a Disciple of Our Lord Jesus Christ," *Ensign,* May 2017.

8.   Thomas F. McDaniel, *Clarifying Baffling Biblical Passages* (2007), 288–292, e-book.

9.   Marily Oppezzo and Daniel L. Schwartz, "Give Your Ideas Some Legs: The Positive Effect of Walking on Creative Thinking," *Journal of Experimental Psychology* vol. 40, no. 4 (2014): 1142–1152, http://dx.doi.org/10.1037/a0036577.

10. M. Russell Ballard, "How to Prepare to Be a Good Missionary," *New Era,* March 2007.

Chapter 11

WHERE DO I GO FROM HERE?

Advice for the newly returned: What to do when you don't quite know what to do

For eighteen months or two years, a missionary lives a life completely separate and differently from the one they lived before departing on a mission. They wake up and go to bed at a standard, prescribed time. They follow a common daily routine. They abide by certain rules from a handbook, some of which may seem odd or difficult to understand. They make daily and weekly plans. They live in an apartment someone else found for them. They get a monthly subsistence allowance that is fixed. They have an assigned companion whom they did not personally choose. They spend most of their time thinking about others, not themselves. They talk to strangers every day. They write emails home about their experiences. They live a structured, routinized lifestyle. Until one day, they go home.

Coming home from full-time missionary service can be as challenging as going on a mission in the first place. In fact, adjusting to life after a mission may be even more difficult than adjusting to missionary life because both the person, and previous circumstances, have changed so much. Returned missionaries must learn to transition from a highly organized life dedicated to service to a new life of work, school, and personal relationships.

"I felt like a fish out of water," Cami said during our returned missionary class at Dixie State University. "The Dominican Republic is so different from southern Utah. I just couldn't relate to anyone or anything for months and months. I felt so lost. I just wanted to go back to serving a mission where I knew who I was and what I was supposed to do each day."

Coming home, returned missionaries must suddenly learn how to live a new life teeming with social media, pop culture, and lifestyles that couldn't be further from strict mission rules. They come back a changed person, and they go into a different world with new expectations they may feel unprepared to meet.

"It's like *The Lion, the Witch, and the Wardrobe*," said Emily, a returned missionary from the Texas San Antonio mission. "In the book, the children go to Narnia and have these amazing experiences. They grow into these powerful, capable adults, and then they come back through the wardrobe. To everyone around them they are still children, and there's no way for them to explain what they've experienced in a way that people who haven't experienced it can understand."

Many recently returned missionaries feel anxious about the new expectations that others have about them, especially when it comes to balancing conflicting roles and figuring out what to do next in their lives. When on a mission, they only had one primary responsibility—to preach the gospel. Now they have many different demands. Figuring things out, however, may seem more important to friends and family than to the recently returned missionary.

Brent, a recently returned missionary from the Texas McAllen Mission recalls, "my Dad and brothers had lots of advice for me about getting a job and what I should do next. But it seemed pointless to me. It already seemed like I had done the most important thing I could ever do in my life. Serving a mission is what I had planned to do ever since receiving the Aaronic Priesthood. So now what? 'Who cares,' I told them. It's all downhill from here anyway. Everything they said to me just seemed so irrelevant."

In the movie *City Slickers*, a trail boss named Curly, played by a crusty old Jack Palance, tells two suburban guys going through a bit of a personal crisis that the secret to life is to do *just one thing*.

"One thing, just one thing. You stick to that and everything else doesn't matter," Palance says.

"That's great, but what is that one thing?" asks one of the guys.

"That's what you gotta figure out," Palance responds.

Feeling the weight of figuring out what their own "one thing" might be can create a lot of anxiety for newly returned missionaries. How will I know it when I see it? What if I get it wrong? Or what if I figure it out too late? A year-long *Deseret News* study found that even in the best of circumstances, today's college students are often overwhelmed and coping with anxiety.

"There's so many important choices I feel like I need to make right now," says Kendra, a recently returned missionary who served in Peru. "I feel overwhelmed at times. So I just don't make any decisions at all. I'm praying, but I don't feel like I'm getting any direction. And I feel so selfish, like now it's all about me. I'm not used to that at all."

While being with a companion twenty-four hours a day was probably one of the more difficult adjustments upon entering the mission field, it can be equally difficult *not* to have a companion to talk to who can relate to all of the things you are experiencing. Many returned missionaries feel a certain uneasiness and loneliness, especially when their friends may have moved physically or moved in a different direction spiritually in their lives. They may not have the same steadying influence of a companion or fellow missionary friend.

SORTING THINGS OUT

While we all like choices, making decisions can be hard. The "pressure" of making a wrong decision can be overwhelming. It can seem to many recently returned missionaries that others have got it all figured out and know exactly what they are going to do next. Since the RM is still trying to figure things out, they figure they must be badly off track or extremely behind. Nothing could be further from the truth. Frankly—regardless of our age or circumstances—most of us are still searching for answers about what to do next. We are all still trying to figure things out in life. While a few returned missionaries do know what they want to do as a chosen career and may even have a girlfriend or boyfriend who waited for them while they were on a mission, but these circumstances are the minority. Most of us are simply figuring things out as we go.

Sometimes it can seem like if we only had more information about a situation, we would certainly make the right decision. This is false! Too often we suffer from "information overload." There is such a blizzard of confusing and conflicting facts—especially on the internet—that are available to us today. Our search to get all of the facts can actually impede our ability to make good decisions. We can never know all there is to know about anything, nor should we try. What's important is not getting all of the facts but instead getting the right and necessary information at the right time. Relevant and timely information is more important than complete and perfect information.

For instance, research on doctors and medical diagnoses has shown that the availability of so much information isn't just a nuisance; it can be deadly. Extra information often isn't very relevant to a doctor's diagnosis and can confuse the issues and delay taking action.[1]

So, what are the implications for returned missionaries facing their own decisions? Spend less time amassing general information and more time considering what's important to you. Then, explore the details of your preferences. Too often, returned missionaries don't have enough breadth of experience to really know what they want to do. They need to *diverge* before they can *converge*.

Diverging is broadening, trying new things, experimenting, and opening yourself up to new possibilities. Too often we stay in our comfort zone and fail to even consider unfamiliar personal, family, or career goals. Missions broaden us in unique but still limited ways. Still, they have likely started us on a road of self-discovery. In returning home, too many returned missionaries simply return to the familiar life they had rather than embracing new possibilities. Do you find yourself putting forth objections to something new or unfamiliar that is available to you?

Do you tend to think that if you can't do something perfectly, then it's better not to try it at all?

Helen Keller, while being both blind and deaf, refused to be categorized by others for her physical limitations. In 1940 she wrote a small book called *Let Us Have Faith* with this famous paragraph:

> Security is mostly a superstition. It does not exist in nature, nor do the children of men as a whole experience it. God Himself is not secure, having given man dominion over His works! Avoiding danger is no safer in the long run than outright exposure. *Life is either a daring adventure or nothing.* To keep our faces toward change in the presence of fate is strength undefeatable.[2]

Converging, on the other hand, opens us up to new possibilities, but they can turn into mere daydreaming unless we take action by eliminating those things which may not suit us. Converging involved making decisions, running down a path, and giving our best efforts without looking back. Robert Frost's famous poem "The Road Not Taken" speaks about not only taking the less familiar path but also making a choice when faced with two really good options. Choosing between diverging paths in the woods is something that demands action. Here's how the poem begins:

> Two roads diverged in a yellow wood,
> And sorry I could not travel both
> And be one traveler, long I stood
> And looked down one as far as I could
> To where it bent in the undergrowth;
> Then took the other, as just as fair,
> And having perhaps the better claim,
> Because it was grassy and wanted wear;
> Though as for that the passing there
> Had worn them really about the same.[3]

Note that each path looked " just as fair" and they were really "about the same." We often face multiple options and may find it difficult to determine which is best. Nevertheless, sometimes they are really "about the same." But deciding and putting our hand to the plow without looking back enables us to make the best of what we have decided upon.

Rather than agonize over your choices or harbor regrets or wonder about the road not taken—go forward with faith. In most cases, almost every decision in life can be revised, sharpened, or adjusted. Making decisions empowers us.

How can you get started? Begin by asking yourself, "What is it that I like to do, and how can I do it as much as possible?" This may take some effort and determination. It is not a casual request. Elder M. Russell Ballard has said:

> I am so thoroughly convinced that if we don't set goals in our life and learn how to master the technique of living to reach our goals, we can reach a ripe old age and look back on our life only to see that we reached but a small part of our full potential. When you learn to master the principle of setting a goal, you will then be able to make a great difference in the results you attain in this life.[4]

First, write down in a journal all the "shoulds" that run through your mind. What are the thoughts that roll around in your head when you think about school and work and life and personal relationships? What are all the things you tell yourself you *should* do, achieve, and be? Should you be married in a year? Know what kind of job or career you want by now? Live in a certain area of the country? Make it personal by writing statements that begin with "I should," or they can also begin with "I need to," or "I have to," or "I can't." "Shoulds" can be sneaky.

Start your list now by listing some of your "shoulds" here:

I should _____

I should _____

I need to _____

I can't _____

Writing creates precision, so don't just think about them out loud. Write your "shoulds" down. Some of these may be important to you, others, not as much. This task serves to identify items on your to do list. These "shoulds" can be externally derived or internally developed. Once you have written them down, you can then decide which ones are more or less important to you. Some of your "shoulds" may not be realistic, or they may create anxiety, or they may be completely motivational. They are not innately good or bad until you decide what you want to do about them.

There is an old baseball story about a newspaper reporter who interviewed three separate umpires to determine how they decided whether a pitch was a ball or a strike. The first umpire he interviewed simply said this to his question: "Some are balls, and some are strikes. I call them as I see them." The second umpire gave the exact same answer as the first umpire. But the third umpire gave a different answer. He said instead, "Some are balls, and some are strikes. But they ain't nothing until I call them."

This applies to the "shoulds" in your life as well. Whether they are important and can help you make better life choices—or whether they are external cultural messages that you can identify and discard—is up to you. By writing them down and then revisiting their importance, you take control. You are then better able to make a conscious decision to focus on certain aspects of your life and adjust your own direction.

GETTING TO KNOW OTHERS

In my final interview with missionaries returning home, typically I would encourage them to get to know a lot of different people before deciding who to marry. It will help you get to know yourself better as well as help you see what characteristics you want in a spouse. Too often, recently returned missionaries feel too much pressure to "find the right one" quickly and get married as soon as possible. Putting ourselves on a strict timetable can be a mistake. As the mission age has been lowered, missionaries are returning from full-time mission service at an earlier age than in the past. It takes time and effort to adjust from returning home after missionary service. Taking the time to get to know many other people will help returned missionaries figure out how to be a better spouse as well as help them find a person with similar interests and values.

Timing matters. Perhaps a twenty-six-year-old returned missionary may need to spend less time getting to know others and more time dating and courting than a twenty-year-old returned missionary who is still adjusting to a post-mission lifestyle. For the recently returned missionary, getting to know others may be the best approach for some period of time.

There's a lot of misconceptions about how millennials are approaching developing new relationships—including dating. With the expansion of dating apps and social media trends, many believe that millennials use mostly online tools to meet new people. While this may seem like a good idea to some, a survey of millennials reveals they don't agree. In fact, less than twenty percent of those surveyed said they thought dating apps were the best way to meet new people. So what did they suggest instead? Almost two-thirds of these young adults said the best way to meet new people is through friends or shared interest groups. So instead of surfing online, realize that others are looking across the room at who is volunteering at an event or participating in a church activity.

Going in a group is the best way to go, millennials said in the survey. It's an easy way to size up a situation, get acquainted with lots of different people, and find out if there is a connection with anyone in particular. It's also a "no pressure" activity that doesn't require anyone to carry the conversation or stick together for a set period of time. It's a great way to get acquainted with a lot of different people.[5]

If group activities aren't happening, initiate them yourself. Organize a group hike, host a game night, have a movie night, or play capture the flag in a big field. It may feel uncomfortable to be the instigator, but most people are just looking for someone to be the gatherer, and they're all in. After those big group get-togethers, once you've identified someone you'd like to go out with, grab a friend, and plan something that you can do together with your dates. Double dates for first dates (or second or third dates) take a lot of pressure off the table. Here are some fun double date ideas: have a pizza making party, hop around town to find the best apple fritter at the donut shops, have a scavenger hunt at the grocery store, picnic in the park, or have a bake-off with the other couple.

Such group experiences—like dating—are the best not only when you want to have fun but also when you have an idea of the type of person you'd like to get to know better. This means having a realistic road map of the values, interests, and attributes that are most important to you in a future partner. Dedicate the necessary time and effort to consider these possibilities and develop a unique list that isn't overly superficial.

Just because somebody is a member of the Church does not mean the person has a testimony of the gospel either. Once you've dated for a bit, begin a scripture study together. Take note as to the other person's thoughts on varying gospel topics. Ask questions about topics that you hold dear or even have questions about, and see how the other responds.

Having a testimony of the gospel, being a strong covenant keeper, and having the desire to start a family is important—vital even—but the good news is that there are plenty of members that possess these sound spiritual qualities. So, what else matters to YOU? Do you want to get to know someone who likes the outdoors or someone who would rather stay inside and play games? Do you like a boisterous, give-and-take atmosphere or something that is more sedate and low-key? More often than not, we don't typically consider these preferences, so we don't have a clue when we meet others if we'd really like to get to know them better or not. Take the time to consider a few of these types of preferences so that you don't get overly influenced by first impressions.

Pay attention to any "red flags" so that you don't get overwhelmed by "chemistry" or romance. It can be tricky to notice controlling or coercive behavior and not ignore it at the beginning of a new relationship only later to have serious regrets about it.[6] This can often happen in new relationships, and sometimes simply becoming more aware of these red flags helps us to deal with them better. While there are various individual compatibility questions that are more easily assessed, here's some "red flags that are too often overlooked:

- Anger issues (like when anger turns physical such as punching a table)
- Controlling or manipulative behavior (like "I'll do this, if you do that." Or "Why don't you put on a different shirt?")
- Not wanting to make a new relationship public (like "I don't want others to know about us yet.")
- Unpredictable or immature behavior (like making fun of people, harmful pranks)
- frequent mood changes (like extremely angry to extremely apologetic)

- Excessive debt/shopaholic (like spending money on expensive things when in school, getting into serious debt)

Too many recently returned missionaries say they feel pressure from family or friends to date enough simply because they think it necessary to find a partner quickly. There are lots of good people who are looking for friendship, love, and marriage in the Church, but too many rush through the process. There is a distinct balance. As Elder Uchtdorf noted in a general conference address, we can be happy marrying any number of persons whose values, interests, and attributes are compatible with our own values and attributes.

> Now, just one word to those of our single brethren who follow the deception that they first have to find the "perfect woman" before they can enter into serious courting or marriage: My beloved brethren, may I remind you, if there were a perfect woman, do you really think she would be that interested in you? In God's plan of happiness, we are not so much looking for someone perfect but for a person with whom, throughout a lifetime, we can join efforts to create a loving, lasting, and more perfect relationship. That is the goal.[7]

Elder M. Russell Ballard speaking at a young adult fireside said:

> We all need time to ask ourselves questions or to have a regular personal interview with ourselves. We are often so busy, and the world is so loud that it is difficult to hear the heavenly words: "Be still, and know that I am God." [8]

Such "personal interviews with ourselves" can help us set goals, clarify values, and make plans that might include getting to know others and developing deep and lasting personal relationships. If you are looking to date someone with specific attributes, make it a goal to be working towards those qualities within yourself as well. Be the type of person you want to marry.

TECHNOLOGY USES AND ABUSES

Young adults both in and out of the Church use technology a lot. It has many uses and abuses. Like so many things, technology is neither good nor bad. It is how we use it—or abuse it—that makes us either well or poorly integrated in both society, and the kingdom of God.

Elder M. Russell Ballard declared that "they need to be our servants, not our masters. For example, if later tonight you share inspiring thoughts from this devotional on social media, your smartphone is a servant. If you randomly surf the Internet, your smartphone is a master."

He expressed concern about excessive text messaging and use of social media that supplant talking directly with one another, and talking in prayer to God. "I also worry that some of you check your email, Facebook, Twitter or Instagram accounts or send text messages during the most important gathering in the restored Church of Jesus Christ of Latter-day Saints, our sacred sacrament meeting," he said.[9]

Some parents and church leaders are worried that young people carry their scriptures and other Church resources on their phones and tablets, "but I am not," he said. This expressed confidence by an Apostle of God in our ability to use electronic devices at church effectively is both a good reminder of our competency and a helpful guide for our Sabbath day worship.

Elder Richard G. Scott in April 2013 commented that having the scriptures on a smartphone provides flexibility—and he offered a specific suggestion on how we might take advantage of their convenience by memorizing scripture passages regularly:

> Who could have imagined not very many years ago that the full standard works and years of general conference messages would fit into your pocket? Just having them in your pocket will not protect you, but studying, pondering, and listening to them during quiet moments of each day will enhance communication through the Spirit. Be wise in how you embrace technology. Mark important scriptures on your device and refer back to them frequently. If you young people would review a verse of scripture as often as some of you send text messages, you could soon have

hundreds of passages of scripture memorized. Those passages would prove to be a powerful source of inspiration and guidance by the Holy Ghost in times of need.[10]

Memorizing scripture passages can be a blessing in many ways in our lives: as reminders, as sources of inspiration, and as pathways to receive personal revelation. Smartphones and social media can give us access to information that previously had limited availability as well as the opportunities for group chats. "Virtual support" was unavailable to previous generations. Text chains enable groups of friends to share inspirational messages or join together in encouraging gospel living in ways that simply were not possible years ago. Technology can transform us spiritually if we use it properly.

Technology also has its limitations. Pornography abounds all over the internet. Stalkers trap unsuspecting persons in webs of deceit. Frauds and hoaxes with misinformation and "fake news" appear on the web. Rather than use this as an excuse to shun electronic devices, Elder Bednar emphasized at the 2016 Mission Presidents Seminar that mission presidents should help returning missionaries learn how to filter and manage images and information on the internet.

As Elder Bednar notes:

Missionaries will one day leave the spiritual seclusion and security of the mission field. We have a duty to help this rising generation learn that the only filter that successfully can overcome and avoid evil resides in the heart and mind of a faithful disciple of Christ. Only the companionship of the Holy Ghost can fortify sufficiently against "the fiery darts of the wicked" (Ephesians 6:16).[11]

The Church's official website provides some helpful suggestions for families to combat the negative influences of the internet, and these suggestions can also benefit recently returned missionaries and young adults in particular. For instance, it suggests recognizing that persons on social media may not accurately portray who they are or what their purposes are in interacting with you. Not everyone on the internet is a friend, and some will not have your best interests at heart. Recently returned missionaries can benefit from discussing these types of issues together with each other to help educate one another, and provide safeguards that members of a group might adopt together. Such topics of discussion, suggested by the Church's website for families, could also be used in an institute class, family home evening group, scripture study group, or even just among a group of young adult friends. Some of the topics include:

- How to handle cyberbullying or inappropriate texting.
- How to create appropriate posts for social networking.
- What to do when noticing inappropriate behavior or images.
- What information or content is inappropriate to share online.
- Where it *is* appropriate to use digital devices.[12]

Such discussions should focus on preventative measures for future problems. Someone may already feel worried and ashamed if they have seen or participated in inappropriate content or behavior. A calm approach will help to legitimize the seriousness of such topics and enable an open discussion that allows all participants to support each other in the appropriate use of technology.

As Elder Bednar noted, the most effective filters are the internal ones we create for ourselves with the Holy Ghost's guidance and direction.[13] Here's a few questions we can ask ourselves to help invite the Holy Ghost to aid us as we seek to use technology appropriately:

- Am I using technology in uplifting ways?
- Am I keeping my personal information safe from others?
- Am I building others up or tearing them down?
- Am I careful about what I share online?
- Am I careful with who I associate with online? [14]

By asking ourselves such questions and discussing them with others, we can use digital tools to expand our search for things that are "virtuous, lovely, or of good report or praiseworthy" as the thirteenth Article of Faith encourages us to do. We can assert clean dominance over our technological lives.

REFERENCES

1. Corey Dean "How Doctors Can Manage Information Overload," *Medical Economics,* June 11, 2019, medicaleconomics.com/view/how-doctors-can-manage-information-overload.
2. Helen Keller, *The Open Door* (New York: Doubleday, 1957), 97.
3. Robert Frost, *Mountain Interval* (New York: Henry Holt, 1916), 3.
4. M. Russell Ballard, "Go for It!" *New Era,* March 2004.
5. Jennifer Boeder, "Would you rather meet your significant other IRL or through a dating app?" The Tylt, July 9, 2018, thetylt.com/culture/meet-irl-or-online.
6. Lisa Aronson Fontes, *Invisible Chains: Overcoming Coercive Control in Your Intimate Relationship* (New York: Guilford Press, 2015).
7. Dieter F. Uchtdorf, "The Reflection in the Water" (Church Educational System worldwide devotional for young adults, November 1, 2009), broadcasts.churchofjesuschrist.org.
8. M. Russell Ballard, "Be Still, and Know That I Am God" (worldwide devotional for young adults, May 4, 2014), broadcasts.churchofjesuschrist.org.
9. Ballard, "Be Still."
10. Richard G Scott, "For Peace at Home," *Ensign,* May 2013, 30.
11. Sarah Jane Weaver, "'Please do not fear technology,' Elder David A. Bednar says at 2016 Seminar for New Mission Presidents," *Church News,* June 30, 2016.
12. "Using Technology Safely," *Prevention and Protection,* (online manual of The Church of Jesus Christ of Latter-day Saints), churchofjesuschrist.org/study/manual/abuse-prevention-and-protection/using-technology-safely?lang=eng.
13. David A. Bednar, "That We May Always Have His Spirit to Be with Us," *Ensign,* May 2006.
14. "Using Technology Safely."

Chapter 12

IN IT FOR THE LONG HAUL

Navigating the road ahead without neglecting where you have been

Coming home from a mission can be hard to do. Katie, who has been home from the Oklahoma, Oklahoma City Mission for a year and a half said:

> The hardest thing for me is still the feeling that I'm not so valuable anymore. I loved being a missionary and feeling that I was a part of something grand, bigger than myself. Then, I came home and I'm just another returned missionary. I've changed, but most people around me are still the same. Some of them want me to go back to being the same as well. I long for that missionary feeling to return again.

There's an old saying that "you can't go home again," which applies to many different types of life experiences, not just returning home from a mission. As Katie noted, she had moved forward in her life while friends and other family members may not have done so. While there's some truth to this saying, it's incomplete. Home is a place that we can always return to even when it's in a different house or with different people. Home is a state of mind, it's in our hearts as much as it's a place.

Still, a mission changes us, and change brings both new perspectives and new demands. We must figure things out all over again when returning home from a mission. Learning how to do so and learning how to do it well enables us to deal with other life transitions that will surely come as well such as attending school, starting a new job, or experiencing the gain or loss of family members.

LIFE TRANSITIONS

When Ben returned from the Peru Santiago Mission, he moved back home to work and go to school. Two years after returning home, he was saving money but giving up a lot of independence.

> I knew moving back home would mean I'd have to give up some things: less independence, less privacy, and my dating life would get scrutinized. What I didn't expect was to be treated like a child again. Seemingly every weekend I had free, my mom expected me to help her out with something. Usually, it was moving furniture, driving her somewhere, picking things up, or fixing something. If I didn't help out, I would be scolded for being lazy or ungrateful. Everything I did was monitored and judged way more than during my mission, and I didn't like it.

Any significant personal change can make us feel anxious and maybe at a loss on what to do next. Following a mission, which is structured with well established expectations, we can become uncomfortable with the uncertainty and ambiguity of post-mission life. All of a sudden, we must adjust to new ways of living, at least temporarily, while figuring out longer term goals and trying to achieve them. All this can leave us feeling completely unprepared, and we may feel confused, upset, sad, or withdrawn.

I experienced all of these feelings and more when I returned home six months early after serving just over two and a half years as a mission president. My wife passed away very unexpectedly when we were nearing the end of our mission. I was released and went home early. Since I had already retired in order to accept our mission call and we had rented our house to a young family in the stake, I was literally jobless and homeless. But what was more painful was that after 42 years of marriage, I returned home without my eternal companion. Now I was the one who had to give up some of my independence and move back in with children and grandchildren until our house became available. Reeling with grief, I had to tell people over and over again what happened. I had to reassure past and current missionaries through social media that I was okay. None of what happened to my wife or to me affected my testimony except to make it stronger. When anticipating a normal release before her passing, I had expected to encourage returned missionaries from our mission for the rest of our lives. We often said to them at zone conferences that we never made a three year commitment to them; we made a lifetime commitment to them. We would always be available to talk about their lives, their families, their Church callings, and quite frankly, everything. When I said all that, I just didn't expect that I would be doing it all by myself. Alone.

It took some time for me to adjust, when returning home from our mission, to figure out in my mid-sixties what life held for me and to go forward with faith. While my circumstances may be somewhat unique, perhaps each missionary's return home and individual challenges are also unique. But there are also some general principles that were helpful to me and to many others that can be useful in adapting to a post-mission life. We will go through these suggestions in the following sections.

EXPECT TO BE UNCOMFORTABLE

Transitions are disruptive and can be confusing. After returning home from a mission, there may not be clear answers for a while to some of life's pressing questions: where to live, whether to work or go to school, how to develop relationships with members of the opposite sex. We may not be accustomed to this discomfort and feel like we are not getting answers to our prayers. We may feel like we are not receiving direct enough answers that we can use to move forward confidently. Such discomfort should not be unexpected; it is normal and natural. Recognizing that it is not an anomaly is the first step in dealing with it.

After discussing the first few months home with many different returned missionaries, many describe it in a similar way. After being home from her mission for only a few months, Jennifer said it this way: "The first few months of being home were dark. It was like I had this dark cloud constantly hovering over me. I felt alone, and I had forgotten where I found purpose and meaning in my life prior to the mission."

Alieen, another recently returned missionary, said it this way:

> Suddenly, from one night to the next, everything you ever knew to be your source of joy seems to be taken away from you. It seems as though nothing you could ever do going forward will ever be as meaningful, and your only responsibility is yourself: not your companion, or your converts, or the members, just you. We repeated our purpose almost daily in the mission field, and then we return to regular life where our purpose is yet to be found. As missionaries, we come to realize that life is so much better when we don't focus on ourselves, but at this point there is no other choice but to build our own lives. It is the breaking point for a lot of RMs.

We often say "time heals all wounds" but time alone doesn't change anything. Instead, doing things changes things. Not doing anything leaves everything the same. We have to change ourselves, and we can learn from the experiences of others how to best do that.

DON'T GET IN A HURRY

Some things take time. While time itself may not resolve certain issues, taking enough time to slow down and deliberately decide what action steps to take is important. Of course, the Lord's advice to Oliver Cowdery as he attempted to translate the Book of Mormon may also apply: "Behold, you have not understood; you have supposed that I would give it unto you, when you took no thought save it was to ask me. But, behold, I say unto you, that you must study it out in your mind; then you must ask me if it be right." (Doctrine and Covenants 9:7–8).

We must do our part to study, investigate, ponder, and decide for ourselves on a course of action, then ask for guidance from our Heavenly Father. We must do our part! We must exercise our agency. We must thoroughly evaluate options, and make a decision, and not expect that by merely asking for guidance the Lord will lay out a course of action for us.

This can be a little scary. It can feel like we have big, important questions for which we need answers and that perhaps getting an explicit, direct, unequivocal answer maybe isn't too much to ask. However, struggling with such questions and making up our mind ourselves is an essential feature of mortality. Sometimes we simply have to come up with our own best decision and simply move forward. Elder Dallin H. Oaks noted that sometimes our strengths, in fact, can become our weaknesses if we expect too much from the Lord and are unwilling to do our part:

> A desire to be led by the Lord is a strength, but it needs to be accompanied by an understanding that our Heavenly Father leaves many decisions for our personal choices. Personal decision making is one of the sources of the growth we are meant to experience in mortality. Persons who try to shift all decision making to the Lord and plead for revelation in every choice will soon find circumstances in which they pray for guidance and don't receive it. For example, this is likely to occur in those numerous circumstances in which the choices are trivial or either choice is acceptable.[1]

TAKE ONE STEP AT A TIME

There is an old saying that states that the best way to solve problems and make decisions is like eating an elephant: just take one bite at a time. Trying to swallow an elephant whole is impossible; taking a bite at a time is doable. Returned missionaries don't have to address and figure everything out all at once. Unpack decisions. Experiment. Dip your toes in the water. Light many small fires. Try new things, but don't bet the farm on any of them. Give yourself room to make mistakes without letting any of them become so big that you can't back up, shift gears, and go in a different direction.

HAVE THE RIGHT FRAME OF MIND

When we are in a hurry, lonely, tired, or upset, we can make bad decisions. It's okay to defer making a choice until you have considered all the options, and have considered your own emotional equilibrium. Ask yourself: Are you anxious? Does this decision feel overwhelming? Are you feeling any peer or family pressure to decide? These can be warning signs that you need to wait a little while to clear your mind and stabilize your emotions. Sometimes we need to slow down to go fast.

USE YOUR SUPPORT SYSTEM

Family, friends, and former missionary companions can all be helpful upon entering your post-mission life as well as through other life transitions, but it can take some time and effort to reconnect, or even revise, your support system when home from your mission. You may need to help them by setting some ground rules in advance, so they don't simply add more pressure or end up giving you unwanted advice. Here's some ground rules developed in a returned missionary institute class which you may find helpful:

- Let me be the navigator on what we discuss; don't take over the conversation.
- Ask me at least twice as many questions as you give answers, help me weigh options.
- Avoid leading or rhetorical questions such as "Don't you think . . .?" or "Wouldn't you agree that . . .?"
- Keep suggestions tentative by offering ideas, not giving mandates.
- Give examples with a range of options; don't fence me in.

- Tell me a story with a practical application; don't disguise something you think I should do.
- Stay on topic; don't give unwanted advice on other matters.

FINDING A JOB, STARTING A CAREER

Among the many new tasks confronted by recently returned missionaries, one of the most pressing tasks is finding short-term work and figuring out longer term career goals. While this can be a little nerve-racking, rather than thinking of it as a "one time decision," instead see it as a process of learning about yourself and about career options that interest you. There is a book on career planning with a title that captures the dilemma of early career planning for a many recently returned missionaries: *Want Experience? Get a Job. Want A Job? Get Experience.* It can be difficult to get a job or experience. The good news is that you don't have to do everything all at once. You can always change your mind. In fact, one of the best things you can do is to avoid making any career decisions too soon. Take the time to explore what you are good at, what jobs you are most interested in, and how your goals can best be achieved.

In Lewis Carroll's *Alice in Wonderland*, Alice is faced with a dilemma about which direction to go when two roads diverge, so she asks a Cheshire cat sitting in a tree for help.

"Would you tell me, please, which way I ought to go from here?" Alice asks.

"That depends a good deal on where you want to get to," said the Cat.

"I don't much care where—" said Alice.

"Then it doesn't matter which way you go," said the Cat.

"—so long as I get somewhere," Alice added as an explanation.

"Oh, you're sure to do that," said the Cat, "if you only walk long enough. . . ."[2]

It is difficult to make choices, especially when it comes to deciding what work you'd like to do for the rest of your life. There are so many opportunities that it's easy to become overwhelmed simply by the sheer number of options. Did you know, for instance, that the *Dictionary of Occupational Titles* published by the U.S. Department of Labor has more than sixty thousand entries? That's a lot of possibilities!

Career decisions are difficult to make, but it is worthwhile to choose wisely. If you can place yourself in a job you enjoy, going to work each day will be a pleasure. If you hate your work, the days will drag on and on. So, what makes the difference? Good jobs and satisfying careers do not just happen. You can't just walk aimlessly in any direction and hope to end up at the right destination. It takes planning and trial and error.

If you can discover something you're good at to begin with, your strivings for excellence are much more likely to produce desired results. Too often people worry about their liabilities instead of working on their strengths.

Keep in mind that talents, skills, and character traits are not just different words for the same thing. You may be instinctively good at using your hands, but you must develop this talent through study and application for it to be useful. For instance, a seamstress may be able to visualize what a completed dress will look like before she even begins to work. However, she must also know how to sew. And she must be familiar with the advantages and disadvantages of various types of material. A nurse may be wonderful in the way she relates to people—patients, doctors, and administrators. That is a talent. But unless she has developed the trait of remaining calm and the skill of providing competent care, you probably wouldn't want her to give you a shot.

For the most part, your talents will lie in activities you enjoy doing. Part of the reason you enjoy the activities is because you are good at them. But having a talent in a particular area does not ensure that you will be successful in a career requiring the use of that talent. It simply means you may be able to acquire skills associated with that talent more easily than others.

A researcher named John Holland identified six basic talent areas and grouped them with occupations that seem compatible.

1. **Realistic.** Involves aggressive actions, physical activities requiring skill, strength, and coordination. Examples: forestry, farming, architecture.
2. **Investigative.** Involves thinking, organizing, or understanding data, graphs, and reports. Examples: medicine, biology, computer science.
3. **Social.** Involves interpersonal rather than intellectual or physical activities. Examples: education, social work, sales.
4. **Conventional.** Involves structured, rule-regulated activities arranged in a logical fashion. Examples: engineering, accounting, electronics.
5. **Enterprising.** Involves verbal activities to influence others to attain prominence or recognition, to achieve collective goals. Examples: management, law, public service.
6. **Artistic.** Involves self-expression, expression of emotions, creativity. Examples: art, music, interior design.[3]

Basically, all talents can be grouped into one of these areas. Ask yourself: What kind of person am I? Social? Artistic? Conventional? That's a key to the type of career you should pursue.

Here's another approach: List all of the jobs you have had (full-time, part-time, or volunteer). Write down the types of skills required to do these jobs well. Have a discussion with someone else who has done the same job to make certain your list is complete. Write down all of the skills you gained from each job.

Now write down the ten most important things you have accomplished in the last five years, even if you didn't do them all by yourself. Write down the skills used to achieve the things you accomplished. Use this list to help you determine what you are good at and what you like to do. Use it to find careers that fit with these types of skills.

INFORMATIONAL INTERVIEWS

An informational interview is an informal conversation you can have with someone working in an area of interest to you using a list of five to seven structured questions. It is a way to get current, up-to-date information on the skills and requirements about a specific job or career field. It is helpful to talk to several people in the career field that interests you, not just one person, so that you can compare answers among various people and not be swayed by a single perspective. You may feel awkward reaching out to people you don't know well. However, most people actually enjoy taking a few moments out of their day to give advice to someone with an interest in their field. Here's a list of common questions you may want to use in an informational interview:

- What is a typical day (or week) like for you?
- What do you like most about your work?
- What do you like least about your work?
- What are some common career paths in this field?
- What related fields do you think I should consider looking into?
- What steps would you recommend I take to prepare to enter this field?
- What skills, abilities, and personal attributes are essential to success in your job/field?
- What advice would you give someone who is considering this type of job (or field)?
- Can you suggest anyone else I could contact for additional information?

There is no one "ideal" occupation you must somehow discover or remain in forever. Many people who have enjoyed one type of job may change their career completely mid-life and find similar satisfaction doing something else. Also remember that as you develop talents and skills, you will be given additional talents and skills. The Lord has said, "And all this for the benefit of the church of the living God, that every man may improve upon his talent, that every man may gain other talents, yea, even an hundred fold" (Doctrine and Covenants 82:18). That simply increases the likelihood of finding a rewarding career.

COURTSHIP AND MARRIAGE

Most missionaries will likely have a transitional period after they return home from their mission. For some this may be a matter of months. For others, this may be a longer period of time sorting through their hopes, dreams, ambitions, and interests. Just as there is a clear adjustment period after arriving in the mission field, so there is a clear adjustment period upon returning home from it. This adjustment period varies from person to person and likely takes place in two phases. First a period of three to nine months simply to get reoriented to the "outside world" followed by a longer period of twelve to eighteen months to figure out longer-term plans and set things in motion for the future.

During this second adjustment period, returned missionaries need to begin *purposeful dating*. A few years ago, Elder Dallin H. Oaks and Sister Kristen Oaks spoke at a Church Education System fireside on "Dating and Hanging Out" and suggested that at some point following a mission returned missionaries should begin *purposeful dating* that is quite different from the *get acquainted dating* they may have participated in before their missions. In this fireside, Elder Oaks said:

> For many years the Church has counseled young people not to date before age 16. Perhaps some young adults, especially men, have carried that wise counsel to excess and determined not to date before 26 or maybe even 36. Men, if you have returned from your mission and you are still following the boy-girl patterns you were counseled to follow when you were 15, it is time for you to grow up. Gather your courage and look for someone to pair off with.[4]

Notice that Elder Oaks, who dated his first wife June for two years before marrying her when he was in his junior year at BYU, suggests that there is a different pattern of dating for young adults than for youth. In this same fireside, he encourages Young Single Adults to consider inexpensive dates and to "shop around" to better understand themselves as well as evaluate compatibility:

> Simple and more frequent dates allow both men and women to "shop around" in a way that allows extensive evaluation of the

prospects. The old-fashioned date was a wonderful way to get acquainted with a member of the opposite sex. It encouraged conversation. It allowed you to see how you treat others and how you are treated in a one-on-one situation. It gave opportunities to learn how to initiate and sustain a mature relationship.

For many returned missionaries, dating will transition into courtship with someone whom you are comfortable with but with whom you are still getting acquainted. This is a time to become open and determine if you are compatible with each other and can develop a loving, lasting eternal relationship. Many married adults would counsel about getting too physically affectionate too soon: it can cloud your judgement and replace developing a deep personal connection with "lip service." For the same reason, don't pray together, or attend the temple together until you have made a decision to marry. Spiritual promptings are individual and are best if they remain personal until a couple decides to marry for time and all eternity.

For those sisters who have fewer opportunities to date and may go an extended period of time without marrying, Elder Oaks had this advice during the same YSA fireside:

> If you are just marking time waiting for a marriage prospect, stop waiting. You may never have the opportunity for a suitable marriage in this life, so stop waiting and start moving. Prepare yourself for life—even a single life—by education, experience, and planning. Don't wait for happiness to be thrust upon you. Seek it out in service and learning. Make a life for yourself. And trust in the Lord. Follow King Benjamin's advice to call "on the name of the Lord daily, and [stand] steadfastly in the faith of that which is to come" (Mosiah 4:11).

SUMMARY

The famous reformer Martin Luther once noted that we can put off getting started with anything new in life an indefinite number of times. He said: "How soon 'not now' becomes 'never.'" Getting started with the rest of your life may be easy or it may be difficult. Regardless of your situation, take charge of your future. There's an ancient Chinese saying that "a journey of a thousand miles begins with the first step." So, get started! Begin by asking three basic questions:

1. **What do I want to do next?**
2. **What is the worst thing that can happen?**
3. **Who can help me?**

No one else can really decide for us what we want to do today or in the future. Ultimately, it is our decision alone. It can be scary making such personal decisions, but we can always readjust and change direction. We don't have to single-mindedly pursue any goals that are unreachable or unrealistic for us. We may not qualify for the Olympics, win a Nobel Prize, or get elected president of the United States. So what? Those are not the only goals worth pursuing. We get to choose what matters to us. We get to decide where to put our time and energy. Make the most of it!

Each of us gets to choose how to build on the experiences of our mission and make our commitment to serving the Lord and others a lifetime commitment. What we do—school, careers, church callings—is less important than how we live our lives by choosing to be engaged in good causes. We must make the most of every single day of our lives following our mission.

> For behold, it is not meet that I should command in all things; for he that is compelled in all things, the same is a slothful and not a wise servant; wherefore he receiveth no reward. Verily I say, men should be anxiously engaged in a good cause, and do many things of their own free will, and bring to pass much righteousness; for the power is in them, wherein they are agents unto themselves. And inasmuch as men do good they shall in no wise lose their reward (Doctrine and Covenants 58:26–28).

REFERENCES

1.   Dallin H. Oaks, "Our Strengths Can Become Our Downfall," *Ensign,* October 1994.

2.   Lewis Carroll, *Alice's Adventures in Wonderland,* (New York: Bantam Books, 1981), 46.

3.   John Holland, "Self-Directed Search," in *Making Vocational Choices: A Theory of Careers,* (Englewood Cliffs, New Jersey: Prentice Hall, 1973), 182.

4.   Dallin H. Oaks, "Dating versus Hanging Out," *Ensign,* June 2006.

About the Author

NORMAN C. HILL

Norman C. Hill is a former mission president in the Ghana Accra West and Sierra Leone Freetown Missions and a former counselor in the Texas Houston Mission presidency. He is the author of six previous books and numerous articles in the Church's *Ensign*, *Liahona*, and *New Era*. He is an Affiliate Associate Professor at BYU's Ballard Center for Social Impact and a former institute instructor. Professionally, he worked for ExxonMobil as manager of training and development and for the Reliant Energy Delivery Group as Human Resources Vice President. He was a Kellogg Foundation National Fellow and serves on the board of directors for several companies and organizations in Sub-Saharan Africa.

Notes

Notes

Notes